LET THERE BE LIGHT

ELECTRIFYING THE DEVELOPING WORLD
WITH MARKETS AND DISTRIBUTED ENERGY

RACHEL KLEINFELD AND DREW SLOAN

TRUMAN NATIONAL SECURITY INSTITUTE

ISBN: 978-0-692-01563-6 (paperback)
ISBN: 978-0-9847814-0-9 (Kindle)
ISBN: 978-0-9847814-1-6 (ePub)
ISBN: 978-0-9847814-2-3 (ePDF)

Credits: Cover photo iStockphoto© BlackJack3D, globe illustration by Michael Rohani, photo-manipulation by RD Studio. Book design by DesignForBooks.com

Contents

Acknowledgments

This little book owes big thanks to many people who were essential to its creation. First, we wish to thank those who labored in the trenches, but whose names are not on the cover. Sarah Beckerman, our intrepid research assistant, found answers to our toughest questions with good humor, intelligence, and amazing skill. She found more than one needle in a haystack—but even more useful, she helped us find the haystacks! This book would never have been written without her help. We are also grateful to Rob Harper, an intern at the Truman National Security Project Educational Institute who helped us begin this project with a set of excellent, all-encompassing memos that let us know the topic had legs before we had fully decided to turn it into a book.

Next, we wish to thank the Smith Richardson Foundation and our wonderful program officer Nadia Schadlow. Nadia's deep experience across the field of international relations, and her openness to new approaches in the energy realm, enabled us to embark on a project outside the mainstream—which we hope will bring crucial ideas into the policy world.

Early drafts of this monograph received excellent feedback from readers, including Virginia Lacy of the Rocky Mountain Institute; Wilson Rickerson, CEO of the Meister Consultants Group; Hisham Zerriffi of the University of British Columbia, Deborah Gordon of Stanford University, and others who read portions of the work. All remaining faults remain ours alone—but these readers who slogged through early versions prevented us from making many more mistakes.

We also owe thanks to the many, many individuals and institutions who spared their time for interviews—especially those early on who took part in our blue-sky questioning before we had honed in on the most important elements of the energy equation. Our appreciation to each of them is deep. However, since some are in sensitive positions in government or overseas, and as not all will agree with every one of our conclusions, we will list them by institution rather than by name. Our thanks to those we spoke to at the Department of Defense Power Surety Task Force, the Office of the Secretary of Defense Task Force for Business and Sustainability Operations, the Task Force Energy, Navy; Army Energy Policy; the Marine Expeditionary Energy Office; Star-Tides and National Defense University; the National Renewable Energy Laboratory—USMC Afghanistan Assessment; the National Renewable Energy Laboratory more generally, multiple departments of the World Bank; the GEF; the Department of Energy; the U.S. Treasury Department; EERE/FEMP; BSO; the Hudson Clean Energy Venture Group; the Solar Electric Light Fund; Stella Group; IDE; other business and nonprofit leaders;

and professors from Stanford University, MIT's Energy Lab, Denver University, and the University of British Columbia; and Caerus Associates.

Specially thanks to Ted Howes and Geoffrey Brown from IDEO, who led an early workshop that helped us see the fragmentation of the distributed generation field, as well as its possibilities. Their unique facilitation clarified a number of issues that receive notice in this book. We would also like to thank the workshop participants, who joined us from the military, development profession, US government, and international financial institutions—many of whom had never been brought together in one room before!

Our thoughts were inspired by muses who deserve mention. Rachel's early interest in energy began over a decade ago in conversations with Jim Woolsey, and visits to his soybean-oil powered farm. Her education in social entrepreneurship began in childhood, fueled by the thick "catalogues" of Ashoka entrepreneurs that arrived at her Alaska home, and blossomed through conversations with hundreds of entrepreneurs in the field. Drew's passion for energy was fueled by the mentorship of Amory Lovins during Drew's internship with Rocky Mountain Institute in 2008. That passion was further edified by conversations with Dr. Rob Stoner of the MIT Energy Lab as well as Dr. Thomas Perry formerly of the National Renewable Energy Lab.

Finally, we dedicate this work to the entrepreneurs making this revolution happen—and all those working to bring light to the developing world.

"If we stop thinking of the poor as victims or as a burden and start thinking of them as resilient and creative entrepreneurs and value-conscious consumers, a whole new world of opportunity will open up."

—C. K. Prahalad, *The Fortune at the Bottom of the Pyramid*

Introduction

It was about 5:45 A.M., right around first light, and I was staring out the back window of an up-armored Humvee. I'd been in Afghanistan for almost four months, and had been in a lot of villages and seen a lot of things—but I had yet to see anything like this. A band of Kuchi tribesmen, their collective existence packed up on the backs of camels and donkeys, were migrating through the countryside. The juxtaposition between me, an American soldier, ensconced and outfitted in modern technology and this nomadic people was startling. They seemed to have been forgotten by time, living in the 14th century instead of the 21st.

Our motorized transport quickly left the slow-walking Kuchis behind. But I continued to think about them as I visited different Afghan villages throughout the day. As I looked around the homes of my Afghan hosts, I wondered just how different their lives were from the Kuchi nomads whose lives, in turn, were so different from mine. There were no lights, no television, no radio. These Afghans lived in houses, but aside from that, they had much more in common with the Kuchis than they did with me.

Later that night, back at our base I stood in a guard tower gazing out at the Afghan villages located nearby. The stars in the night sky were bright, much brighter than I remembered them back in the U.S. I realized with a start that it wasn't just my memory: The stars really were brighter, because there were no lights on in the Afghan villages, no stores open, no streetlamps to prevent crime, no TVs with their bluish hue to bring in impressions from the rest of the world—nothing illuminated to compete with stars for dominance over the darkness. At that moment, I realized that the Afghans in those villages, and the Kuchi tribesmen I had seen in the morning, were living in the dark in a manner and a reality almost completely forgotten not just by me, but by all of us who exist primarily in the modern world. And that literal darkness—with its attendant lack of jobs, impoverishment, no connection to the rest of the world, and limits to education—was one of the causes of the instability and insecurity that had such dire effects on America on 9/11—and which we were there to fight.

I was riding on the back of a motorcycle along a bumpy dirt road, deep in rural India. In the driver's seat was a sugar farmer who had created a network of schools to beat the immense poverty that surrounded his village in Uttar Pradesh. Now he was taking me to live in one of the schools, which would be home base while we met with hundreds of micro-entrepreneurs his organization was helping. It was the year 2000—but the view of the countryside was biblical. Women crouched by the side of the road, using hammers to break rock into smaller rock. Small children swarmed across a brick-kiln yard, shaping clay into bricks by hand. Straining their thin necks, they piled four at a time on their heads to carry to the ovens. Men as thin as walking-sticks worked the fields, toiling for paltry wages that kept them in debt-bondage to the landlords. Their instruments of agriculture were hand sickles and oxen-drawn carts. We were in one of the most populous places on earth at the dawn of the 21st century—but where was the industry? Where were the factories? I found my answers when we got to the school. As dusk fell and dung-fires began to haze the landscape, my host proudly turned on a diesel generator—specially rented, for me, the village's honored guest. It was the only reliable electricity in the region—a locale that housed millions. And it was only there for the length of my stay.

As I visited hundreds of small entrepreneurs, talking with them in their tiny barbershops, viewing their sewing handiwork, asking about the profitability of their bicycle-repair shops, a realization dawned. Micro-credit for these, the poorest of the poor, would keep their families alive. But without electricity, they could not scale. The capacity of their hands limited their industry and hard work. They couldn't call other markets and price their products fairly—there were few landlines, and they had no way to charge a cell phone. Water for irrigation or industry had to be drawn by hand, with no electricity available to fuel an automatic pump. The dawning and setting of the sun created stark bounds for their working hours, and for the schooling of their children.

—⚡—

As authors, we came to the field of distributed energy and market-based development solutions from different paths, to say the least. Drew is a former Army officer who served in Afghanistan and Iraq before getting degrees from Harvard Business School and the Kennedy School of Government and entering the energy field. Rachel worked in development and the rule of law before getting her Ph.D. and founding a national security organization that trains America's political and policy leaders in 21st-century security issues. But over time, these worlds converged. Rachel visited the heart of Afghanistan, Pakistan, and Bangladesh and worked with military-service members returning from tours in the toughest parts of the world. Drew spent time at the National Renewable Energy Lab and Rocky Mountain Institute. We both became interested in energy in the developing world when we realized that its absence was a vital matter that concerns our national security, our world, and the human potential of more than one and a half billion people on earth. Bringing energy to these parts of the globe needs to enlist more than our do-good, charitable impulses. It requires the seriousness of purpose called for by a national security need—and the scaling abilities of our nation's most ingenious businesses. That is what this book is about.

As America wraps up one conflict in Iraq and ends a decade in Afghanistan, providing reliable electricity has become a crucial measure of operational success in the battle for "hearts and minds." In Iraq, General Petraeus asked daily about the success of a particular electrical tower—knowing that electricity had become a symbol to the local population of whether America could deliver.[1] In Afghanistan, the Taliban is siphoning electricity and electrical fees to shore up their rule in parts of the country under their control.[2] Where counterinsurgency is the method of battlefield success, providing electricity to an unlit community—and even more important, restoring electricity to a community that has lost it—is a more significant tactical triumph than taking a hill.

But we are not only concerned with areas in which we are at war. The method with which the developing world generates its energy is also of concern for those focused on the threat-multiplication effects of environmental refugees and resource conflict.[3] Coal currently fuels approximately two-thirds of India's electricity[4] and nearly as much in China.[5] The vast consensus among the scientific community strongly suggests that the greenhouses gases associated with such production will exacerbate severe weather events on that continent. And even for those who dispute human agency as a cause of weather changes, the effects of changing climate patterns and resource scarcity are already manifesting themselves. In Africa, the increasing lack of firewood is resulting in small-scale skirmishes right now. India is already constructing a fence to keep out Bangladeshis they expect to be displaced by rising water. In nearby Pakistan, the situation is even more dire. Severe summer flooding in 2010 resulted in one-fifth of the country being submerged, and forced millions of refugees into makeshift camps, leaving them ripe for radicalization by Islamist charities helping them with their material needs. Pakistani poverty and the government's failure to provide basic services such as electricity constantly undermines the stability of that nuclear-armed state.

Climate instability will compound the problem. Closer to home, Central American governments are facing devilish resource decisions. For instance, in Guatemala, drug and gang violence overflowing from Mexico and Columbia now causes more deaths annually than occurred during that country's civil war. And through connected gang affiliations and gun-supply routes, the violence has spread throughout the United States. Yet as climate change creates increasingly severe weather, the hurricane-battered isthmus must decide between rebuilding decimated infrastructure or building more effective police forces, secure prisons, and educational resources to reduce gangs.[6] If we want to save our military forces, police forces, and lift capacity for our security needs, and not create greater requirements for deployment to assist humanitarian disasters, we need to mitigate the likelihood of increasingly severe weather events. The continued confluence of energy poverty and misguided energy production in the developing world represents not just a direct threat to the people living in these areas, but also a real threat to the developed world.

The lack of energy in the developing world is part of a new set of problems that occur where human insecurity meets national insecurity. These new challenges, from water scarcity to failed states, were once dealt with by development professionals, humanitarian organizations, and charitable groups. They have now become front-and-center issues for national security and defense thinkers. And their intersection creates an urgent need that we ignore at our own risk. But traditional development-aid or government-diplomacy models are not enough to address these new problems. Instead, governments, social-sector organizations, and businesses must each play a role to meet these new security challenges.

A SCALABLE, MARKET-BASED BUSINESS MODEL FOR DISTRIBUTED GENERATION

A few prescient political leaders have recognized the importance of getting reliable energy to the developing world. Most have sought to address the need through big-ticket electricity generation programs. Huge dams for hydropower, electricity grid extensions, international carbon caps, and other large-scale, big-impact solutions are all under discussion at the United States Agency for International Development (USAID), the U.S. Treasury Department (through its work with international financial institutions), and the U.S. State Department. The $7.5 billion dedicated to Pakistani aid in the first Kerry–Lugar bill, for instance, included a priority focus on energy provision through centralized, government-utility–run plants that would take years to come to fruition—if they ever do.[7] USAID has a $1.2 billion dollar fund for building a modern electric grid in Afghanistan, but its plans to construct large-scale, fossil-fuel burning power plants have yielded very little power.[8]

This focus on energy makes sense: But to get where we need to go fast enough and at a large enough scale, the means must change. We believe that the biggest impact can be attained by small-scale but widely adopted energy systems, in the form of distributed generation—solar, wind, and other forms of energy—that don't require hookups to a national grid.[9]

Like the ubiquity of the cell phone versus an old-fashioned call center, or the pervasiveness of the laptop versus 1960s mainframes, small, distributed solutions can have massive impact if scaled and widely adopted.

As with most good ideas in the developing world, the devil is in the details. Grand theories falter in implementation time and time again. Our purpose is not simply to argue for distributed generation as a method—but to offer a model for implementing the change. Our suggestions for how to create scalable, market-based implementation for distributed generation draw on insights from the adoption of other technologies in the developing world—and provide a business model that could work for other sectors that wish to spread and scale in that ripe, but difficult, business environment.

A new implementation model is needed, because the old one has failed. Over and over again, well-meaning aid organizations have simply given solar panels, small dams, and other distributed generation technology to the poor, hoping to provide help. Over and over again, their efforts have left behind micro-hydro projects that have become silted and corroded into oblivion and solar panels that are used only as expensive roofing materials. By ignoring the need to market and create demand, failing to ensure ongoing funds for maintenance, and other predictable, repeated oversights, the common model of providing free or subsidized distributed energy generation to the poor has shown its ineffectiveness. At worst, it leaves behind failed relics and poor-quality technology that taint the image of distributed energy for a whole generation. At best, it helps a single village at a time—but, dependent on massive subsidies, foreign expertise, and an external labor force for installation and maintenance, it fails to scale. In no instance has the subsidized "technology drop" approach met the vast need for energy in the developing world.

But there are effective ways to spread and scale distributed generation. One only needs to look at Afghanistan—where one-third of the population has purchased a cell-phone contract in the past decade—to know that new technologies can spread across even poor, war-torn countries with amazing speed.[10] Drawing lessons from market-based business models that spread other new technologies can help us harness new ideas that have proven their effectiveness in scaling other innovations across the developing world.

Our point is not that the market is a perfect vehicle: It is not. A pure market model cannot succeed. The distributed energy market is too nascent for businesses to survive alone—it needs bilateral and multilateral institutions to help governments reduce tariffs and create a benign regulatory environment that does not disadvantage distributed energy. It needs social-sector organizations more interested in social good than maximizing profit to train technicians, installers, maintenance workers, and otherwise create the human capital businesses needed to help the new market thrive. Businesses require capital to scale—but since risk-averse banks balk at supporting small and medium-sized enterprises, this capital is most easily gained from multilateral banks, or social enterprises looking to break even rather than gain the vast rewards that usually match such significant risk. It needs advertising and education to persuade people that a particular product is worth their hard-earned money. And even after a scalable market has been created, with channels for distribution, installation, and maintenance, some people will still be too poor for the reach of the market and will then need some subsidy or assistance.

However, a market-based solution that takes these other needs into account has real potential. More than just potential, this type of model, where the social sector plays a role in generating demand and the private sector exists to supply a product, has already been proven. Technologies from cell phones to home construction materials to distributed generation itself have reached hundreds of thousands of people through this method of market-building. It is this model—one that develops an ecosystem of public, private, and non-profit cooperation to focus on first stimulating demand and desire and using that to spur growth and development of supply—that we will examine in the hopes that its further implementation can yield real success on a larger scale.

The next chapter will discuss why the current state of energy access is increasingly detrimental to the developing world and to our own interests, and will introduce what we mean by distributed generation—and the promise it holds.

But if it's so great, why hasn't it taken root already? Chapter Three looks at the challenges that have kept the distributed generation of energy from scaling to date, and offers business-model suggestions for meeting each of these obstacles.

Chapter Four provides a short review to focus on the most underappreciated obstacle to uptake and the key behind the business model we advocate: generating demand. To those of us who see energy as necessary as food and water, the need to market electricity may seem counterintuitive—doesn't everyone think they need energy? But for those groups who have done without for thousands of years, generating demand is a crucial part of creating a business market. We consider other cases of products that haven't made it in the developing world despite "obvious" need—such as the failure of cheap PUR water-purification tablets—and those that have succeeded in gaining widespread adoption.

Once a product is demanded, a market can start supplying it. But selling to the poor is not easy. Chapter Five draws on case studies of products, from shampoo to cell phones, that have been successfully sold to the world's poor, to draw lessons for the energy market. We see three important business-model innovations: dividing products into smaller, affordable units; collective financing; and turning a product from a cost to an asset. While all three are important, none is more crucial than the insight that for a product like energy to really take off in the developing world, it should be targeted at those who will use it as an income-creator.

A new business market cannot be created in a vacuum. Chapter Six expands its lens to the entire market environment, looking at how an ecosystem of businesses, social-sector organizations, financial institutions, and multilateral organizations can meet the other obstacles described in Chapter Two. We then look at how energy companies have met this need and other needs by thriving within a market friendly environment.

The seventh chapter applies these lessons to Afghanistan, where success could make a palpable, immediate impact in our current counterinsurgency—and to the lives of millions of the poorest people on earth. As the quip goes, if we had a choice, we wouldn't start from here! But Afghanistan happens to be the country in which the U.S. government is focusing 120 billion dollars a year in resources—and an equal amount of attention. It is currently investing some of those billions in infrastructure, and its nascent programs in the energy sector are pointing in the wrong direction, and need to be turned around quickly. While far from the ideal developing market to experiment with these models, Afghanistan is a possible market for distributed generation— and we think that creating a market-based system for energy delivery will prevent major problems caused by overly subsidized, "technology dumps" that can have significant negative unintended consequences, but are the main model now being used in that country.

Finally, in our Conclusion, we give our thoughts on how distributed generation can make a major impact on the developing world, with a description of the lessons of successful, scalable business models and a breakdown of the roles that businesses, social-sector organizations, and government and intergovernmental bodies can best play to bring light to the world.

"Since I got the solar I get a lot more custom[ers] in the evenings. People come in to watch TV after they've finished working in the fields. I'm very happy with the solar, it's going to make me some money! Once I've paid this one off, I'll get one for the home." [Interviewer: Do you have any problems with it? Can you understand how it works?] "No, there are no problems. . . . I take care of it, I've got the manual. And of course I can understand it! Women can understand these things, we're not stupid—we've got a woman prime minister after all!"

—'Pinky', café owner, India

Why the Energy Gap
Is Your Problem, Too

From a mud hut in India, a tendril of smoke rises at dusk. The evening sun filters through a thin brown haze, as charcoal and animal-dung fires are lit in each home to cook the night's meal. These small fires—perhaps supplemented by a kerosene lantern—will be all the energy the village has to heat their homes, boil water for dinner, and provide light. In the town an hour away, diesel generators thrum through the night. Their loud engines deafen, and black smoke chokes passersby. But what can they do? Even the town lacks a central source of electricity, and diesel generators provide the only light for the roadside tea houses.

This is energy poverty. It is daily life not for a few hundred or thousand individuals, but for more than 1.5 billion people, or almost one-fourth of the world's current population.[11] Not everyone living in energy poverty lives in a small village. Some reside in cities and simply do not have electrical connections or face constant power outages, as in megacities from Lagos, Nigeria, to Mumbai, India. However, about

85% of that 1.5 billion people live in remote areas that are difficult to connect to centralized power grids.[12] They are disconnected for multiple reasons: Geography, economics, and security all play a role. These are people completely "off the grid." And there are a lot of them.

Fortunately, current estimates by the International Energy Agency (IEA) project that by 2030, even with no new policy or development measures put in place, the percentage of people living without access to electricity will be almost half of what it is today.[13] That would be a remarkable achievement. However, given population growth, that would still leave 1.3 billion people—an amount roughly equivalent to the entire current population of China—literally in the dark.[14]

There's no doubt that this lack of energy is tragic. Yet there are many sad realities in the world. The question is: Do numbers such as these matter, and, if so, why and to whom? The issue of importance is not a casual one. People have survived by burning animal dung or wood (biomass, to energy wonks) for thousands of years. Meanwhile, America has many problems to address—why should the needs of remote countries occupy policymakers, when so many Americans want their leaders focused on needs at home? Electricity for small huts in remote locales seems a minor issue, easy to put off and unlikely to destabilize a region in the way that, say, ignoring terrorism in Pakistan might. Perhaps energy in the developing world should simply fall into the "nice, but not necessary" box that kills many a good idea.

It *is* easy to dismiss the problem. But it would be unwise. Like receiving a diagnosis of cancer, then coming home to find your kitchen aflame—you undoubtedly would want to deal with the fire first, but using it as an excuse to put off treating your cancer indefinitely would be dire. Energy poverty matters: to those living with it, and to those of us in the developed world. Here's why.

THE CHALLENGES FOR THE DEVELOPING WORLD: HEALTH AND HUMAN PRODUCTIVITY

Energy poverty leads to a staggering loss of health, life, and productivity around the world.

But it helps to put this loss in context. Consider this: Aid groups and governments have spent well over $6 billion dollars in the last decade to stop malaria.[15] They have drained swamps, distributed mosquito nets, and even funded research to create a biologically engineered mosquito that is unable to carry the virus.[16] This is all undeniably good. Malaria causes up to a million deaths per year.[17] Yet according to the World Health Organization (WHO), indoor health pollution resulting from the burning of solid fuels in homes leads to more than 1.5 million deaths a year. Indoor air pollution, in other words, causes half again as many deaths as malaria, nearly as many casualties as tuberculosis, and half as many as HIV/AIDS—but very little is being done to stop it.[18]

Poor women and children—those who are relegated to cooking chores inside the home, and who live in less-ventilated conditions—bear the burden of most of these deaths. And the costs go beyond deaths.[19] In the developing world, indoor air pollution causes roughly 36% of the lower respiratory infections, and 22% of the chronic respiratory disease.[20] A child exposed to this kind of indoor air pollution is two to three times more likely to catch pneumonia. Evidence exists that conditions such as low birth weight, infant mortality, asthma, cataracts, and tuberculosis can all be at least partially attributable to indoor air pollution resulting from the burning of solid fuels in poorly ventilated areas.[21]

Meanwhile, the macro-effects of all this burning of dung and wood has repercussions far beyond villages and homes where such energy is used. An "Asian Brown Cloud" composed of dense pollution from these dung and wood fires combined with the massive coal plant output in Asia is visible from satellite images and is estimated to be more than two miles thick and six million square miles broad—the size of the continental United States. The cloud, first spotted in 1999 by researchers funded by the National Science Foundation, affects respiratory health throughout Asia, and was implicated in a 2002 study about negative effects on the water cycle and crop growth. This is a serious problem for development in countries whose population growth already outstrips their ability to provide food for their citizens.[22]

In other words, the costs of poor health are not only born by those who cough, suffer, and die. With large numbers of people suffering poor health, a country's educational levels, income levels, and GDP are all kept artificially low. Countries lose immense productivity. The world loses the unique talents and the abilities of millions of individuals.

The world particularly loses the talents of women. Not only do the costs of burning cow dung and kerosene disproportionately fall on women, but when electricity and energy is available, it is women who are the most liberated from drudgery—stumbling in the dark to make the morning fire, pounding corn or wheat that would otherwise have been ground in a factory, washing clothes by hand. Reliable electricity reduces the time required for many household tasks, whether that electricity is entirely supplied by the home, or is channeled to small businesses where women can wash or purchase foods that have been slightly more prepared. Electricity enables women to put their own energy into more productive uses and frees 50% of the population to use their talents to contribute to the economic growth of their countries.

DEFORESTATION, DESERTIFICATION, AND CLIMATIC THREAT MULTIPLIERS

The shadow cast by the Asian Brown Cloud points toward broader effects of energy poverty that extend beyond the individual. Climate change, caused in part by the poor energy choices used by the developed world for years, is now driven even more by the pace of energy need in the developing world. China is the world's largest greenhouse gas emitter. The amount of coal burnt in much of Asia means that as electricity demand grows, as predicted by the International Energy Agency and anyone watching the population rising in that part of the world, carbon emissions will also grow. These carbon emissions will contribute to the climate change that is already exacerbating severe weather, such as the floods that put one-fifth of Pakistan under water in 2010. Climate change will create winners and losers: And many of the expected losers happen to be in the most volatile parts of the world. As Bangladeshis and sub-Saharan Africans become environmental refugees, crossing boundaries and entering other countries illegally in the search for resources to support their families, resource scarcity will become a threat multiplier.

For those who don't believe in human-caused climate change, we can look to more immediate and visible side effects of energy choices: deforestation and desertification. Most deforestation in Asia is caused by commercial users and agriculture—things that distributed generation cannot address. However, in other places, such as parts of Africa, millions of homes cooking with wood is a larger cause of deforestation than commercial use. Dead wood is used up quickly, and fuel demand requires ever more cutting down of live trees. The amounts used are staggering: in Africa, 90% of all wood removal is used for energy purposes.[23] Since diesel generators run on fossil fuels, which are one of the few alternatives for energy production, the use of wood for energy is closely tied to fossil fuel prices: When diesel oil goes up, more wood is collected. Such a correlation bodes ill for the future.

Deforestation has serious local and international effects. In mountainous areas, the loss of trees triggers landslides that destroy farmland and lead to an ever-wider circle of poverty. Where farmland isn't buried, soil fertility becomes so degraded that the region can no longer support plant life and becomes, in essence, a desert environment. This cycle of desertification, most notable in sub-Saharan Africa, means that the land not only can provide no energy, but is no longer arable, either.[24] Nor is this process necessarily slow and long-term. In the span of five years, from 2000 to 2005 when oil costs were particularly high, Nigeria cut down 55.7% of its primary forests.[25] Studies suggest that parts of the Sudano–Sahelian portion of Africa will experience severe shortages of fuelwood by 2025.[26]

The human security costs are also serious. In many countries and in refugee camps where wood is the primary fuel source, women and children (those generally tasked with foraging for such supplies) spend up to one-third of their day collecting and transporting firewood.[27] They do not only lose time. Many face brutal rape or kidnapping by guerrilla armies as they venture ever farther from their homes for more scarce resources.[28]

This is where human insecurity starts to meet national security dilemmas. The Sudano–Sahelian portion of Africa where many of these rapes and kidnappings take place happens to lie on a fault line between Muslim and Christian populations.[29] In this and other energy-impoverished areas of the world, families are forced into competition that often breaks along tribal, religious, or ethnic lines as they search for wood and other energy resources. A major study on causes of conflict in this region discovered that the *main* cause was access to scarce natural resources, which outweighed political, religious, and domestic conflicts put together.[30] But these natural-resource fights easily attach to and escalate into broader conflicts of identity that pull others in, creating spirals of conflict in some of the world's most volatile places.

THE CHALLENGES FOR AMERICA: NATIONAL SECURITY

"Climate change will provide the conditions that will extend the war on terror."

—Admiral T. Joseph Lopez, former Commander-in-Chief,
U.S. Naval Forces Europe, and former Commander-in-Chief,
Allied Forces Southern Europe

Environmental refugees and conflict over resources are nothing new—in fact, finite resources are probably the oldest and most reliable source of mass migration and conflict. Relocation to find scarce resources is older than the tale of Joseph's family packing up for Egypt during the Biblical drought. In modern times, Asia and North Africa, both religiously volatile locales, boast a large percentage of the world's climate refugees.[31]

The issue today is that conflict over resources is overlaid by growing terrorist trends. In 1993, American soldiers died in Mogadishu while spearheading a global response to the humanitarian crisis borne out of the explosive combination of unrelenting drought and poor governance. The subsequent collapse of the Somali state, combined with growing Islamic militancy and scarce resources, have kept America involved in combat operations in the Horn of Africa for nearly two decades, trying to mend the instability fracturing the region. And it is in places like Somalia that the call of the Shabab youth is radicalizing even American youth.[32] In fact, the entire Horn of Africa, where fundamentalist leaders capitalize on resource scarcity and conflict to gain new recruits, is an area of such security concern that the United States created a Joint Task Force Horn of Africa in 2002 to address terrorist threats emanating from the region.[33]

But one need not look to environmental refugees, or even conflict caused by climate change, to see how a lack of reliable electricity in the developing world creates national security challenges for the United States. Further instability is the last thing the United States needs in nuclear-armed, terrorist-prone Pakistan. But in the fall of 2011, rioters angry over electricity shortages burned government buildings and battled police, bringing multiple cities to a halt. The opposition leader Nawaz Sharif claimed that the rioters were more dangerous to the government than the jihadist group known as the Haqqani network. The government's solution to the energy crisis is more failed centralized generation—in the form of a hydro-electric dam in Kashmir. The dam, however, would be located on disputed territory claimed by India—a further cause for conflict between two already volatile countries.

Developing world energy choices also create instability by propping up oil-rich countries that oppose the United States. In most of the developed world, oil and electricity are separated, with oil used largely for transportation, and electricity generated mainly by coal, gas, and other fuel sources. In the developing world, however, diesel generators fueled by oil generate the majority of electricity generated by those who are off-grid. The millions of familiar generators kicking up smoke in cities and villages add to the global oil market that enriches oil-rich countries such as Iran, Russia, and other states inimical to U.S. interests.[34] Reams of research show how oil sales entrench dictatorships and autocracies. The correlation is clear: Of the 22 countries that derive more than 60% of their GDP from oil, all are dictatorships or autocratic kingdoms.[35] The causation appears to be the traditional resource course: When governments have major sources of revenue that do not derive from taxation, they are prone to rent-seeking, corruption, and ignoring citizens' needs for economic development. Even when they are not clear enemies, these countries endanger U.S. security because countries that provide no legitimate outlet for political voice tend to spur violent terrorist movements, a tendency noted not only by academics, but also by our nation's leading military academy, West Point.[36] The regimes' desire to maximize their sources of wealth, and citizen anger at the same, leads to repression; repression leads to radicalization, guerilla movements, and terrorism—shake, stir, repeat.[37] Autocracies are also more likely to experience internal conflict and to spur conflict with their neighbors and other countries.[38]

Meanwhile, lack of electricity itself has become a particular obstacle for America in the fight against global extremism. In immensely energy-poor Afghanistan, as we discuss later in the book, the Taliban and NATO forces are engaged in a cat-and-mouse game over who can control electricity—and thus win the hearts and minds of the population. In a counterinsurgency, the population itself is like high ground in a territory-based war—it's what you are fighting for, because the population's allegiances will ultimately decide who wins the war. For that reason, the DoD wanted to provide distributed energy to Helmand Province, where the Taliban were resurgent, to prove to the people that NATO and the Afghan government could give them a better life than the insurgency. The Bush White House forced the DoD to pour $100 million into doubling the capacity of one of the few centralized power plants in the country. The Taliban, however, gained control of some of the distribution, collected payments door-to-door, and cut off electricity to those who refused to pay the Taliban as well as the government for the power. Meanwhile, the Taliban is also fighting for hearts and minds using the same strategy—extending the power grid to villages they control (though stealing, rather than creating, the original energy). At the same time, the Taliban is using power distribution to increase their political standing. For instance, they disrupted these powerlines six times between January and July of 2010—each time, forcing NATO to talk with them.[39] In this way, the Taliban are adeptly transforming literal into metaphorical power. Distributed generation is one way out of this deadly game.

The link between electricity and the fight against terrorism is not confined to Afghanistan's Helmand Province—
in Iraq, Yemen, the Horn of Africa, the Philippines, the
Sahara, and other regions around the globe radical Islamists
prey on vulnerable populations, and America is engaged in
their conflict. Each of these fights are counterinsurgencies,
where governments trying to retain control of their territory
are undermined by insurgents fighting to control their own
areas. For countries throughout the developing world that
are engaged in conflict, providing electricity is one means
to bind citizens to their government and persuade them that
their government can deliver.

Yet delivering on this goal is difficult, in part because we
are turning to the wrong answers. In Afghanistan, despite
recognizing the problem, in nearly ten years neither the
government, nor American forces, nor NATO troops
have been able to ensure a reliable electricity supply, even
in Kabul alone. Nor is failure in this matter isolated to
Afghanistan. In Iraq, General Petraeus recognized that supplying energy was crucial to winning the hearts and minds
of Iraqis. The terrorists had the same realization—and they
targeted energy infrastructure to prevent the state from providing services that would gain citizen allegiance.[40] But the
Department of Defense was focused on a centralized solution: rebuilding the existing electrical grid, which had fallen
into severe disrepair. Rebuilding the grid was slow, however,
since decades of sanctions had prevented replacement parts
from getting into the country while decades of underinvest-
ment in basic upkeep meant that engineers were not just

fixing recent war damage, but were forced to rebuild largely from the ground up. Meanwhile, because the grid was centralized, every time a portion started to get better, terrorists could simply attack a substation and drive it offline again. They could even target their attacks to particular neighborhoods in order to exacerbate the anger of various sectarian groups. General Petraeus diagnosed the correct problem; however, lack of thought about potential electricity options led to a suboptimal solution. When America ended combat operations in Iraq, seven years after entering the country, the country still lacked full power.

Another option is available. Distributed generation—or decentralized energy—is simply not on the radar for many Americans. However, in situations where an electrical grid is likely to be a prime target of terrorist attack, distributed generation offers immense possibilities, proving itself orders of magnitude more resilient than centralized systems.[41] Because distributed generation does not require large-scale infrastructure or government purchasing, it also has the ability to circumvent government corruption, bureaucratic red tape, and engineering difficulties that keep more than a billion people without access to electricity in the developing world. Distributed generation—if provided in ways that scale—can play a major role in U.S. security and in U.S. development policy. But to make good on this promise, distributed technologies must scale. And scaling can only be done by creating a market, where the purchasing power of the poor, rather than the charity of outsiders, drives supply. Giving away these technologies for free—whether through aid, or battlefield commanders' strategic funds, actually destroys markets, and can stop the spread of these technologies to those who need them most.

But before we get to the "how," we must first discuss the "what"—what IS distributed energy, and why would it solve some of the problems we're facing, from development to modern warfare?

THE PROMISE OF RENEWABLE DISTRIBUTED ENERGY TECHNOLOGIES

Distributed generation is a term with many definitions. We use it here to refer to energy creation that is not centrally dispatched. Diesel generators, in other words, are distributed energy technologies.[42] But *renewable* distributed generation, our particular focus, would exclude diesel fuel and include technologies that only minimally enhance global oil markets or exacerbate global warming. These include everything from micro-hydropower to small wind turbines, solar, geothermal, and some non-centrally dispatched minigrids. Renewable distributed generation could also refer to energy produced from biomass and biofuel—though if one goal is to reduce climate impact, these fuels must be chosen carefully.[43]

Distributed generation generally refers to energy solutions that produce less than 20 megawatts per system (very loosely, enough to power about 5,000–6,000 U.S. homes for a year), though it can refer to larger systems in some definitions. We use distributed generation to include everything from a micro-wind turbine that supplies off-the-grid energy to a single Mongolian yurt, to a small dam supplying hydropower to an entire village linked by a mini-grid unconnected to a centralized grid system.

For centuries, all energy that was produced was distributed. Wood stoves, for instance, or individual coal ovens were a main way people got their energy. But in the 20th century, distributed energy was replaced by centralized power plants fueled by coal, gas, and other sources brought from other parts of the country, or even from overseas. Centralized technology had a mass scale that enabled mass development where it was implemented. These grids became the backbone upon which America, Europe, and others built the modern, industrialized world. They became so successful that most policymakers forgot about other ways of producing energy.

Because of the great success centralized power has produced in the past, it is the main model the international community tries to replicate throughout the developing world. However, in the developing world, centralized power's drawbacks take center stage. Developing countries are, by definition, poor. While it is true that centralized generation provides power that is generally cheaper than distributed generation on a per kilowatt and per kilowatt-hour level (without taking externalities such as the need for security or construction into account), centralized plants require a tremendous amount of initial capital in order to be constructed, and significant sums to be sustained and to expand. Even where donors pay for the cost of the initial plant, developing countries are left with systems that they cannot perpetuate when international assistance is reduced. In Nigeria, for instance, only 19 of the country's 79 power plants are operational, resulting in blackouts that cost the Nigerian economy roughly $1 billion a year in economic losses.[44] Political failures, corruption, and mismanagement plague centralized power in many developing countries. At least those plants got built in the first place; millions of dollars in debt relief currently provided to Africa revolves around forgiving loans made to construct power plants that never made it off the ground.[45]

Most developing countries have rural populations that are costly to reach over difficult terrain such as mountains and jungles. Yet centralized generation requires miles upon miles of transmission lines to connect the generation facility to the locations that need the power. Finally, many developing countries are buffeted by war and guerrilla insurgency, as well as endemic theft and a lack of rule of law.[46] Centralized plants themselves, as well as their transmission lines, are easy targets for attacks and theft, and are vulnerable to the severe weather that plagues many developing countries (weather that is projected to get worse with climate change). When these problems affect distributed generation, they can stop electricity generation for a few homes—when they hit centralized plants, they may halt electricity to an entire neighborhood, village, or region. Moreover, they are more likely to affect centralized generation, because it has more infrastructure for severe weather to knock out, and because the lack of individual ownership means that no one is watching to deter attack and theft.

Finally, the way in which centralized power is built is one of its handicaps. Oxfam, the World Bank, and other development leaders are increasingly making the case that underdevelopment is fueled by poor governance, not just poverty—and that corruption is a major cause of such underdevelopment.[47] While our model of scaling distributed generation relies largely on the market, centralized power is nearly always built through large government contracts, or contracts issued by a government-supported utility. Such contracts are ripe for corruption, which plagues large construction projects of all types, especially in the developing world.[48] Meanwhile, markets themselves are a strengthening force for democracy, when these private enterprises push to keep corruption at bay—a central thesis of the Center for International Private Enterprise, which has contributed a quarter century of work trying to help strengthen democracies by building strong markets.[49]

Distributed generation's strengths lie precisely in the areas of centralized energy's weaknesses. Though solar panels, micro-wind, and other locally generated forms of energy still cost more than a diesel generator initially, they are relatively cheap to install. Since distributed generation doesn't require government purchasing—particularly in the market-based model we advocate—it avoids fueling corruption. Generating power next to the user, works with, not against, geographic realities, and is more resilient than centralized generation: Human attacks or natural disaster might affect one household or at most one village, but not an entire region of a country. And as pilot programs in India have shown, when personal or community ownership is built into the distribution or financing model, it leads to local policing of the infrastructure, reducing theft and corruption.

Distributed energy produces other positive social side effects. It moves resources out of the capital city to help smaller urban areas and rural populations—a significant need in many overcentralized developing countries where living in the capital city, or another major city, is the only way to ensure access to some of the perks of modernity. Joint ownership of an energy source can also tie communities together across tribal, sectarian, or caste lines. Counterinsurgency expert David Kilcullen has noted that models where multiple villages must pool together to purchase distributed energy resources can help build social networks and the ownership necessary for locals to police the resource themselves—as shown in the Indian pilot projects mentioned earlier. Clare Lockhart of the Institute for State Effectiveness has also written on the social capital and growing writ of the government that blossomed in Afghanistan from distributed energy projects undertaken through the National Solidarity Program.[50] These are significant benefits with real meaning in the developing world, where, as Robert Putnam noted, a trust deficit may be a crucial cause of underdevelopment.[51]

A PATH TO SELF-RELIANCE

But one of the most exciting realities of distributed generation is that it offers a path for self-reliance to the poor themselves, as well as to poor countries. As companies are beginning to realize with the explosion of "marketing to the bottom billion" books and conferences, the poor have significant collective purchasing power; they simply do not have up-front capital—a topic we discuss in detail in Chapters Four and Five.[52] While many people lack access to the energy grid, or can't afford the up-front cost to purchase a roof-covering array of solar panels that can run into the thousands of dollars, their energy needs are so great that they run kerosene generators and jury-rig dry cell and car batteries at a cost of several dollars per kilowatt hour: orders of magnitude higher than most electricity costs, which are well below a dollar per kilowatt-hour in the same regions.[53] The World Resources Institute estimates that poor households living on less than $3,000 per year spend an average of nearly 10% of their income on energy; other estimates suggest the number is closer to 12%.[54] That average, while high enough, obscures market segments—for instance, the founders of d.light, a solar-light company that markets to the developing world, found that in the markets they were targeting 15% to 20% of household income was spent on light alone—just one part of the electricity market.[55]

Individually, these costs are insupportable: The poor are forced to purchase unreliable, unhealthy energy at a back-breaking cost. Yet collectively, they represent an opportunity: The World Bank's World Resources Institute estimates that the "Base of the Pyramid" market for energy among those earning $3,000 per year or less was $433 billion per year in 2005 dollars—and it could count at least $228 billion of this market worldwide through direct survey data.[56] Compare entry into this market with others: For instance, the entire global soft drinks industry was estimated to be $307.2 billion in 2004, while the worldwide cosmetics industry was about $230 billion in 2006.[57] These are big markets, and big business. The bottom billion energy market is bigger. What Muhammad Yunus, the Nobel Peace Prize–winning leader of the Grameen Foundation which popularized micro-credit, did for financing, distributed generation can do to energy: transform more than a billion people from alms-takers to owners. Distributed generation can empower the poor with a means of production that they can produce, operate, and afford at less than the cost of their current energy expenditures. In other words, distributed energy is financially viable, and scalable through private purchasing power—once more innovative business models are employed.

Yet if distributed generation is such an obvious, scalable solution, why hasn't it already solved the problem of energy poverty in the developing world? Why are nearly 1.5 billion people still without power? After all, we have had solar panels for decades. The technology for wind power and micro-hydro are all well-known. With so much money invested and so much need, why does the developing world remain so energy-impoverished? That is the topic of our next chapter.

On January 2, 2010, north India
plunged into darkness. For hours, industry
stilled, train and plane travel malfunctioned,
and cities from Delhi to Kashmir froze. Deep
fog in the Punjab had overwhelmed the
country's power grid, leaving hundreds of
millions without heat or light in the dead of
winter's cold and darkness.[58]

Assessing the Scope of the Problem:
What Doesn't Work with
Electricity Generation, and Why

Since the birth of modern development aid more than sixty years ago, bringing electricity to the developing world has been a priority. So why, well into the 21st century, are billions still forced to do without?

THE PROBLEMS OF CENTRALIZED POWER

In the 1950s and 1960s, lack of power was considered a major obstacle to development, and large centralized power projects were darlings of international financial institutions such as the World Bank. Large dams that could power nations were considered particularly good opportunities: Hydropower is one of the world's most efficient energy sources and often provides the cheapest energy. In Brazil, hydropower accounts for nearly 85% of all electricity; the Aswan Dam in Egypt electrified 60% of the country when it was first established.[59] An OECD study of just 50 of the more than 500 dams built by the World Bank found that they replaced 51 million tons of fuel annually, in addition to enhanced irrigation and economic benefits.[60] But such large, centralized projects also had significant unintended consequences. For instance, the same OECD study found that resettlement of hundreds of thousands of people plagued more than half the projects. Moreover, water resources change over time—the dwindling Nile River now provides only 8% of Egypt's water.[61] These problems, along with environmental, health, and other side effects, caused the OECD to find only 13 of the 50 dams acceptable from a cost/benefit point of view, with another 13 unacceptable, and the remainder requiring additional mitigation measures.[62]

These social costs are not the only negative externality of centralized power. When energy is generated centrally by utilities, the utilities are often subject to political interference (and are sometimes even unilaterally taken over by national governments, leaving foreign investors bereft, with negative knock-on effects for other foreign direct investment).[63] In democracies, political decisions on pricing such as subsidies that benefit protected industries or important voting blocs are common. The accumulation of such decisions has distorted markets, leading to energy theft, wasted energy that reduces power for other sectors, and stunted energy investment and grid growth worldwide. India, for example, chose to subsidize agriculture by under-pricing electricity and water (which requires electricity to pump). By creating pricing structures tilted against urban industry and the urban poor, they curried theft; approximately half of all electricity generated in India is not paid for, due to theft (which accounts for about one-third of the losses) and subsidy—a direct result of pricing decisions that were made politically.[64] Power companies generate electricity at a loss and collectively lose approximately $4.5 billion each year, ensuring a lack of investment in electrical infrastructure.[65] Hence, while India has centralized electricity and a grid that reaches most of the country on paper, in practice rolling blackouts plague cities and villages alike and the country loses billions of dollars in wasted productivity every year. India is a worst-case scenario for public policy; China, for example, loses only about 3% of its energy to theft.[66] But autocracies and dictatorships create their own problems. Centralized grids enhance centralized power. According to Professor Bruce Bueno De Mesquita of New York University, Mobutu Sese Seko, former dictator of Zaire (now Democratic Republic of the Congo), insisted on a centralized power grid so that he could cut off electricity to any region or town that defied him.[67] He also used centralized power projects to steal—from his people and from aid donors. In 1981, after garnering a billion dollars from multiple donors to build a 1,100-mile powerline to the Shaba copper-producing region, the power was finally turned on—for just eight months. Shaba was already self-sufficient in power; Mobutu and his cronies had simply been siphoning off funds from the project for themselves.[68]

These problems of political economy are, ironically, the upside of centralized power: At least in these cases, some electricity was being generated. In many cases, centralized plants fail to get built at all. The social and political effects of large-scale power plants have generated political and human rights movements that have blocked many pending projects. Regardless of one's opinion of the grievances, their existence has made the expansion of major centralized power projects slow and problematic in many developing countries, in the same way that political backlash has stymied the development of nuclear power in the United States. In many cases, energy is delayed for decades. In some cases, large centralized projects generate so much opposition that they are never built at all. For instance, Enron tried to build a plant that would generate more than 2,000 megawatts of power for Maharashtra, India, and cement U.S.–Indian trade ties. The gigantic Dabhol Power project required tariff changes in India, government loans, insurance guarantees, and political arm-twisting from the Clinton Administration, and an agreement from the government of Qatar to provide liquefied natural gas (LNG). A decade later, following political jockeying, citizen protests, and police brutality against protesters, LNG prices continued to skyrocket above market rates for other substitute fuels, as market observers had warned when the project began. The plant, in which Enron had invested $900 million, was mothballed.[69] By this time, Enron had been dramatically "mothballed" as well, though not, of course, as a direct result of the Dabhol debacle.

Politics are not all that impede the actual construction of centralized electrical projects. As discussed in the last chapter, time and again centralized projects that look terrific on paper are delayed and then destroyed by the realities of developing countries. All such countries are poor, by definition. Many are also saddled with a number of knock-on problems: low-skilled labor forces, difficult-to-traverse countryside, and frequent war or low-level insurgency. Each of these problems has a significant impact on the practicality of centralized energy. Centralized generation requires significant up-front capital investment—saddling developing countries with debt decades before they begin operation, if they begin at all. Miles of transmission lines must link these generation facilities to the locations that need the power—lines that require technical skill and significant financial wherewithal to construct across desert, jungle, mountain range, and other problematic terrain. Electricity is always lost as it travels along distribution lines from the centralized grid to the local user, even in developed countries—but in developing countries such losses often run as high as 20% to 30% due to inadequate maintenance and investment in distribution systems.[70] Large sums of money and large construction projects attract corruption, in production and distribution. Meanwhile, in many countries thieves strip and sell the copper wire from centralized transmission and distribution systems. Guerilla attacks and severe weather diminish system effectiveness. Finally, extending grids to rural and sparsely populated areas is often economically prohibitive. Without votes to drive electrification, autocracies are particularly loathe to electrify beyond ego-driven projects in capitals, leaving large sections of the developing world literally and figuratively powerless.[71]

DISTRIBUTED POWER: NO SILVER BULLET

In the face of such problems with centralized power, distributed generation seems like such a good idea. So why aren't solar panels, micro-hydro turbines, and little windmills ubiquitous throughout the developing world? In fact, these technologies *are* being used in country after country. Distributed energy projects are under way on a broad range of scales using a wide variety of technologies. China is currently engaged in a significant effort to distribute photovoltaic (PV) panels throughout 20,000 rural villages.[72] Wind power is being tested throughout the wind-plains areas of Asia and Southeast Asia as well as in other regions. In Mongolia, the government is disseminating 50,000 micro-wind and photovoltaic systems for nomadic herders, and is providing financing to enable herders to purchase their own systems.[73] In China's Inner Mongolia, the government is also providing 160,000 small wind turbines.[74] Countries as diverse as Egypt and Sri Lanka are also testing this technology at the village as well as the household level. Nor are all such projects government-funded. In Kenya, unsubsidized photovoltaic systems compose 75% of the solar market, largely in dense farming areas—a success we explore in upcoming chapters.[75]

Micro-hydropower has been tested in multiple, often mountainous areas, as well as in China, which is a world leader in this technology. In Nepal and Peru, renewable, distributed energy has been introduced in part as a strategy to deflect insurgency from Maoist and Shining Path elements, respectively, by giving the people what insurgents claimed could only be obtained through violence.[76] Other types of distributed energy under consideration include: wood-gasification from locally produced stoves that can be assembled using local labor; other biomass systems that use waste products but reduce harmful gases released in burning; and local biofuels in India (where the Pongamia plant produces ten times the oil of the equivalent amount of corn) and Africa (where the indigenous Jatropha plant is being tested in Tanzania, although some controversy surrounds the attempt) that could fuel diesel-powered generators.[77]

However, judging by the billions of people living without access to energy on a consistent and reliable basis, distributed generation is not scaling. What's the problem? For simplicity's sake, the variety of obstacles can be boiled down to five areas: financing, government regulation, technology, human capital, and demand.

FINANCING

Most distributed generation programs founder on the problem of financing, which is why it is the focus of our fifth chapter. Financing obstacles take multiple forms, so let's begin by breaking down the problem. First, businesses interested in selling distributed energy to the developing world need capital to produce, market, and distribute their product. Yet banks, the traditional means of attaining business capital, often balk at these projects. Second, in poor markets, households and businesses wishing to purchase distributed generation often need some form of consumer-focused financing to enable the initial purchase and ongoing upkeep of the technology. Consumer financing can include various instruments of credit—but generally, solving this side of the financing dilemma requires a product designed for affordability in the first place, a savvy business model, *and* some form of consumer credit. In other words, for business to succeed in this market, they must create a product and business model that solves the consumer financing needs—and then persuade their own capital providers to provide them with money to begin production.

Why is financing so hard for distributed generation businesses to attain? After all, centralized power in the developing world requires financing, too—in fact, it requires orders of magnitude more up-front capital. But international financiers have decades of experience pricing centralized power generation, and can draw on time-tested models for expected cash flows—even if such projects often founder in reality. They are also often lending to multinational construction companies with long-established track records. Meanwhile, the local power companies are frequently government-subsidized or public utilities without the same financing hurdles.

Major companies such as General Electric are working on distributed generation—but most are focused on the developed world, where barriers to entry are lower. Those companies trying to produce and market distributed energy to the developing world are likely to be smaller, entrepreneurial startups. These companies can go to banks, but many banks see the distributed energy market as untested. Moreover, banks in the developed world often do not know how to price the risk of, say, a solar-panel distribution business in southern Africa, and most entrepreneurs lack the collateral that could back a traditional loan. With so many distributed projects paid for with aid, subsidies, and by nonprofit groups, financial institutions lack a track record for commercial distributed generation. In the conservative world of international finance and global financing institutions, many renewable energy technologies still carry with them significant technology risk.

One would think that businesses that start in developing countries would have it easier. After all, local banks make nearly all their loans to businesses in the local environment. A bank in Uganda or India must already price in the risk of doing business in their own country to lend to a local restaurant or shop—distributed generation should be just another local loan. And while some developing markets may be capital-poor, others, such as China, are well-known for having banks with immense resources to lend. Yet, in some countries, connections are more important than business plans for gaining access to capital. In other cases where small and medium-sized enterprises want to enter the market, they may lack major assets for collateral—the type of clients many developing country banks refuse even for more traditional businesses, such as restaurants and shops. Meanwhile, the energy market is so nascent that it is hard to model returns. Cash flows are based entirely on how the system is designed, and there are few working systems with historical records of performance from which to model loans.

Venture capitalists can fill this gap for entrepreneurs in many sectors where the rate of return may be spectacular enough to justify a riskier investment. But venture capitalists like to see returns within a few years, generally—and those returns must be large. The energy market in the developing world is huge, and returns are likely to be significant—but they are also likely to be slow, since selling to the poor is, by necessity, a low-margin business that makes its money through scale, and scale takes time. Transaction costs are high, since renewable energy projects vary individually to a significant extent in terms of resource assessment, citing, permitting, etc. These transaction costs are even higher in the developing world, where a simple permit—which is often required in greater numbers in developing countries for even simple businesses—may require walking through dozens of offices and vast quantities of red tape, not to mention bribery.[78] So most venture capitalists look for easier places to put their money.

Commercial financing is a significant, but not intractable, problem. Intergovernmental organizations, governments, and social-sector organizations are looking at providing technical assistance to assist local banks with risk models for loans and financing, realizing that this is a fairly common problem for new businesses in developing countries and not unique to the energy field. Meanwhile, a number of social-enterprise financiers have sprung up to address the need for financing among businesses that are for-profit but also carry social benefits. E+Co, the Acumen Fund, and a number of other entities blend business and nonprofit functionality to offer "patient capital"—with investors who expect a longer lag time on return, or are willing to garner lower returns on their investments in order to support riskier businesses with social externalities. Such entities are no silver bullet for small-scale entrepreneurs. Most of these funds are just gearing up themselves, and in order to prove themselves, they focus on the more mature part of the market space, offering capital to businesses that already have a proven track record and simply need to expand—not to the startups. They still solve some part of the financing dilemma. But entrepreneurs trying to create a scalable product are generally forced to raise funds among angel investors, a tough job. A good business plan can founder if no one on staff is a "salesperson" who can sell the plan to those who may be moved as much by emotion and personality as by rational rates of return.

But it is not impossible. Investor groups of angel investors in the social-enterprise space are growing. In stories throughout this book, we share case studies in which local businesspeople, international venture capitalists, private-equity firms, and low-profit international financing firms are helping businesses obtain needed financing to get to scale.

Any capital provider, from a bank to an angel investor, is going to look for a business plan that addresses the other main financing obstacle for selling to the poor: how consumers can afford to purchase the product. For renewable distributed energy, consumers have to bear the biggest cost up front. Although the wind, sun, or water provides its power for free, the initial purchase of solar panels, a wind turbine, or other technology can be quite expensive. As mentioned in the last chapter, the poor are used to spending stunning amounts for substandard power; up to 10%–12% of their total income goes to energy.[79] However, despite this large amount of overall spending, the poor have difficulty amassing the up-front capital needed for the initial purchase of most distributed generation technology.

Moreover, once the initial purchase has been made, the costs may not end. While renewable energy uses free fuels (such as the sun or wind), or low-cost fuels (such as local biofuels), more complex systems such as micro-hydro have ongoing maintenance requirements, batteries run out, and systems can break. These "follow-on" costs have been the bane of many a donated renewable energy system. Too often, the owners of the donated systems either lack the capital necessary to maintain and fix their systems or simply don't know where to go to get their system maintained or fixed (or can't afford to get there). These unfunded maintenance costs are what led one USAID official whom we interviewed to state that as a rough estimate borne of his own experience, 80% of systems that required a battery to stabilize fluctuating renewable supply—which certainly includes PV systems and wind—will fail or have failed and will largely go unrepaired.[80]

Such financing dilemmas are not rocket science: There are many ways to address them. At one end of the market, distributed generation can be attempted at a village or other multi-user level to support larger-scale energy while distributing costs. In Manila, for instance, when the government privatized the market, Manila Water found that one-third of its franchise area had no water at all, and of those areas that did have water two-thirds of the revenue was being lost due to illegal connections, leaks, and faulty meters, while water pressure was low and often stopped altogether. Collecting payments from low-income households was hard—so the company gave locals three options—they could have one meter per household, one for every three or four households, or one for bulk water that would serve 40–50 households. The last two schemes reduced costs to the villagers by up to 60%—and gave them a way out of low-pressure water and at times no water at all. Group-level purchasing, from schools to prisons, took off.[81] In the energy sector, village-based decisionmaking and in-kind contributions have been tested in the National Solidarity Program in Indonesia and the National Solidarity Program in Afghanistan and have demonstrated greater accountability and reduced corruption.[82] For such large-scale distributed generation, an anchor business client may serve as a generator of enough extra energy that the business can also be the power provider for households through a micro-grid.[83] A micro-grid can allow village-level storage and movement of energy, connecting local households without them having to invest in or wait for a connection to a national grid. Micro-grids operate all over the world, from community-maintained and -supported grids in Sri Lanka, to utility-owned grids in Peru. In many cases, they are jury-rigged locally—and are hardly worthy of the name "grid." A solar or wind system owned by an entrepreneur might be connected through a series of plug-ins strung across streets or over roofs to a few other households or businesses nearby. The result is ugly, and if demand is too high, the system simply shuts down—but it works better than no energy at all. In other cases, micro-grids can be quite professional, providing employment to skilled locals. In 53 of India's rural islands, for instance, the Rural Energy Cooperative Society built small power plants of up to 100 kilowatts to fuel villages of 400–500 families.[84]

At the other end of the market, businesses focus on providing energy to individual households. For instance, if businesses offer manageable monthly payment plans, a common strategy in Bangladesh's distributed energy sector, the poor can spread a large up-front cost over many months so that it is manageable. Renting equipment is another method that has been proven to work at the individual household level in some cases.[85] For example, social entrepreneur Fabio Rosa runs a program in Brazil that rents photovoltaic technology along with tamper-proof lights and cell-phone chargers to the poor for $10 a month—a dollar less than the average amount rural consumers were previously spending for electricity.[86] As with most rental equipment, breakage and maintenance costs are borne by the distributor and paid for out of profits. Of course, adaptations on the business-model side require payment collection and financing expertise that add to business costs, and which need to be built into business-financing plans.

As in *Goldilocks and the Three Bears*, we advocate for a middle-option—focusing not on villages or on individuals, but on selling to local businesses. Studies have found that distributed generation projects are most sustainable when they are built to provide enough generative capacity to fuel cottage-level industry that can pay for maintenance costs and the initial infrastructure purchase. Often such businesses have excess energy available for sale to nearby households.[87] While micro-credit, lending groups, and other social-payment methods used for hundreds of years in many countries won't fund individual households that cannot generate any revenue to pay back the loan, they can finance business loans. Such existing, and often traditional, community financing methods can fund up-front costs for many businesses; though they are of less use for day-to-day maintenance that requires small bits of ongoing financing rather than a lump sum.[88] Businesses can also create innovative business-to-business models. For instance, in Chapter Five we discuss Fenix International's ReadySet—a distributed energy source where the company partnered with cell-phone companies to purchase and distribute their product. The cell-phone companies can afford the up-front costs for the ReadySet, and can then distribute them to their retailers, who can use the energy themselves as well as resell power in much smaller increments to individuals who need to charge up their cell phones and other goods. Fenix International gets a reliable customer base that can afford its products, while the cell-phone dealers (small and medium-sized enterprises that are generally locally owned) make money on the energy sales. Meanwhile, the cell phone companies make money on the greater number of messages and minutes used by customers whose phones are charged.

As we discuss in the next chapter, there are significant benefits to introducing distributed energy technology to businesses in which the cost is an investment that is soon repaid, rather than to households for which the cost is a net expense. Once enough businesses in an area have invested in the technology, a business environment can scale to bring down the costs of installation, maintenance, and so on to the point that wealthier, and then poorer, households can enter the market. Market segmentation is an important lesson of successful business models that can work for distributed generation.[89]

Financing *is* a problem for distributed energy, a problem that development aid and nonprofit organizations have tried to overcome by simply delivering free or highly subsidized equipment. We believe there is a more scalable model: creating businesses that sell affordable products to the business-to-business market. But for any such market to exist, it may require changes to government policy, which we turn to next.

GOVERNMENT REGULATION

Good regulation requires a careful balancing act. Markets need some regulation to function well. And since most regulation, even in countries such as Afghanistan, has been built around centralized generation of energy, governments often need regulatory changes to unlock the power of distributed generation. However, poorly designed regulation kills markets. In nearly every country, power companies are either publicly owned or highly regulated. While few countries have laws that prohibit individual household-level power, regulations created to favor utilities may make microgrids or even cottage industry–level power difficult to build, insure, or finance. Regulations tend to be loosely applied in the developing world. But while small-scale, individual-use projects may be ignored, in many countries as soon as someone starts making money from an enterprise regulators become interested—whether for the good of society or for their own enrichment.

Governments also disadvantage distributed generation through subsidies for nonrenewable fuels. In an effort to help the poor, many countries in the developing world have instituted hefty subsidies on everything from diesel fuel to kerosene and propane. Even candles are subsidized in some countries![90] These subsidies distort the market, making it difficult for unsubsidized energy products to effectively compete, even when they would otherwise be less expensive when expenses are calculated over the lifetime of the initial technology and fuel costs. For distributed energy to grow in areas where there are subsidies on fossil fuels, such subsidies may need to be removed.

Import tariffs are another way that government policy can inadvertently harm the distributed generation market. The introduction of import substitution in the 1960s and 1970s left many developing countries with high tariffs in an effort to protect domestic industries. Some of these tariffs may be particularly targeted at distributed energy—but most are more general, and are simply trying to protect local markets against a host of foreign imports. The side effect of such taxes is that goods that must be imported are more costly—sometimes so much so that the tariff alone makes a market-oriented solution impossible. Some developing countries, such as China, have large enough industrial bases and internal markets to build their own solar panels, wind turbines, and generators for dams. But most countries need to import such items, and tariffs, or even uncertainty over taxation, can kill small businesses with low margins.

Last but far from least, a side effect of government regulation is corruption. For every hoop that must be jumped through to bring distributed generation technology into a country or to set up a small energy business, there is the possibility of a palm to be greased. Whether demanded by government regulators, or advanced by businesses in an effort to speed transactions or avoid higher taxes, corruption drives up costs for the end user. Such corruption acts as a tax on the importer or distributor, making prices higher for extremely price-sensitive consumers. For micro-grid projects, they can imperil the entire enterprise.

Getting government regulation right is a tough problem. But it is not insurmountable. In general, markets take off when regulation is rewritten to allow more competition, enable more forms of enterprise, or lower barriers to entry—whether

in the telephone, airline, or energy industry. In many countries, businesses themselves lobby to change government policies. In the distributed energy sector where such businesses
do not yet exist, they can hardly amass the power to affect
laws. Changing government regulations is a crucial job that
must be done by governments themselves, usually assisted or
pushed by bilateral and multilateral institutions, often with
the help of local businesses and social-sector organizations.
Their efforts can be assisted or spearheaded by groups such
as the Center for International Private Enterprise, which
helps businesses organize and advocate for such market-based
solutions. It is not easy—but it has been done successfully in
countries such as Tanzania, in the energy sector, and throughout Africa and Asia for cell phones and in other industries.
The World Bank has produced excellent ideas on handling
regulation that can serve as models for moving forward.[91]

TECHNOLOGY

At a recent meeting with a wealthy investor in America's
solar industry, the conversation turned to this book we were
writing on distributed generation. "What a good idea," the
man exclaimed. "I'll bet we could donate much of our first-
generation or slightly damaged equipment and make a real
difference to the developing world." A well-intended senti-
ment—but this solution is part of the problem.

The poor lack money—not intelligence. They want things to
work, and they often highly value reliability: After all, one
hardly wants to spend an entire year's income on something

that breaks! Their risk-aversion to new technologies is partially based on living so close to the margin: One wrong purchase with the tiny amount of discretionary funds they have, and a poor family may face starvation.[92] Thus, one significant problem that has impeded the market for distributed generation in the developing world was the early distribution of substandard technology.

In country after country, early adopters who spent considerable savings to install their villages' first solar panel or micro-hydro system became laughing stocks when such technology failed a short time later. Such failures could be financially devastating to those who had spent life savings on such equipment—and were highly dissuasive to others. Even if such systems were given away for free, examples of breakage and lack of reliability impeded an eventual market from taking hold. Damaged solar panels serving as immensely expensive roofing material provide visible reminders of a technology that has failed. Such reminders last for decades or even generations through the stories being passed along in small, close-knit villages. They continue to hold back distributed generation markets in much of the developing world, even though technology has greatly improved in the years since.

Technologies must be feasible for local geographies: A wind turbine must be able to be transported across the potholed, washed-out paths that link villages in much of the developing world. Solar panels require sun. They must also provide what the market demands. For example, many nonprofits have tried to provide stoves to the rural poor that mitigate lung damage; but healthier heat sources that fail to burn hot enough to cook tasty food in traditional ways are simply disregarded.[93] **Any energy is not better than no energy**—no one wants to become dependent on a technology that is unreliable, or cannot generate the power they need. Finally, the products must also be able to be fixed by local people, with easily available parts.[94] If a geothermal unit breaks down and cannot be fixed with local labor, or if parts take months to arrive from afar during the coldest part of winter, what will be the demand for geothermal units? You guessed it—zero.

Again, none of these barriers is impossible to overcome. Better technology now exists; it just has to be introduced and marketed—a concept so often overlooked that it's the subject of our next chapter—so that higher-quality products are well-known. Local technological solutions are an excellent use of R&D dollars that governmental and social-sector organizations can provide. Such local innovations as the solar home kits developed by Grameen Shakti for Bangladesh have a track record of success that we discuss in the next chapter. In fact, the hardest of the technological obstacles to overcome is likely to be the memory of poorly functioning products that made their once-proud owners into village jokes.

HUMAN CAPITAL

One of the reasons that functioning systems break and go unrepaired is the lack of human capital in the developing world—in this case, a force trained to fix distributed energy systems. Time and again we read case studies about a well-meaning project providing a village with a working hydroelectric system or windmills, only to hear a year or two later that systems were unmaintained or broken, with no one knowledgeable enough present to fix them. The more complex the technology, the more human capital becomes a problem for creation and particularly for maintenance.

Much has been made in the distributed generation literature of the problem of trained human capital for maintenance. How can such technologies take hold in countries where basic education is minimal? We actually think this is a bit of a red herring. Nothing is as impressive as the technological know-how on display in the developing world when a technology is desired and needs to work. Even villages with almost no literate adults have an auto mechanic and numerous bicycle repair shops, with skills honed over years of practice. The spread of cell phones and similar equipment has led to cottage industries of local repair shops. Anyone who has spent time in developing countries has stories of technological ingenuity—the car engines held together by duct tape, string, and the brilliance of an Indian driver; the replacement fan belt fashioned out of twine by an Afghan jenga truck driver, the thresher crafted out of spare parts held together with sheer ingenuity; the radio that has been deconstructed and reconstructed to work with electricity stolen from a powerline hanging over a slum. This is not to romanticize the lack of resources in such places, or to suggest that the solutions such amateurs attain are the best of all possible means. But it does suggest that where there is a real desire to keep a piece of equipment functioning, the local human capital is often up to the task.

Of course, the simpler a distributed generation system is, the more likely that people on the ground will be able to maintain it. Illiteracy and innumeracy are serious obstacles to education for maintaining more complex systems. But across the poorest parts of the world there are governments, social-sector organizations, and vocational schools that can help with the specifics of this learning process. In fact, when a business area becomes profitable, businesses often train their own sales forces, and private technical schools find they can charge students to learn a profitable skill. Social-sector organizations and government-supported vocational schools can play a very useful role in train-the-trainer programs that catalyze a local work force. To ameliorate the chicken-and-egg problem, such training programs can incorporate multiple skills useful across other sectors that already exist, as well as continuing education to cover the nascent distributed technology sector. Another way around the human capital problem is to use technologies similar to those already in use in the developing world—such as modifying car batteries to serve as the battery storage systems for distributed energies, since villages the world over has someone who can fix cars. The bigger issue, we believe, is the desire to learn—not ability. And this brings us to issues of demand.

PSYCHOLOGY OF DEMAND

One of the reasons the Prius was designed to "look different" was to give Prius owners a sense of status for buying a hybrid car.[95] The much-hyped, two-wheel Segway failed miserably in mass-market sales because its owners hadn't counted on the stigma of driving one—instead of being seen as cool, Segway users were seen as geeks, or as lazy people who didn't want to walk.[96] Status is a key driver of human behavior, and one not to be overlooked by people trying to sell new ideas. Distributed energy may be falling into this trap. Some members of the Western distributed energy community have commented that government ministers in the developing world turn down money for distributed generation. They want centralized grids—like the developed countries have. They do not see distributed energy as a "leapfrog technology" like cell phones—they see it as a lesser technology, and they don't want to relegate their countries to second-class status. Thus, when asking for funds to electrify their countries, ministers tend to dismiss distributed generation. Of course, there may be more venal reasons: Corruption can be simpler in large projects with large contracts to be had. But the psychological factor of demand generation—whether for government ministers, small businesses, or individuals, should not be overlooked.

It was in Afghanistan that one of our authors saw her first videoplayer embedded in a car's passenger side sun visor. Cell phones cover that country—generally with better coverage than we receive in many cities in the U.S.—despite relatively high costs. Motorcycles are common throughout Africa. In slums across India, a television set is generally the first item purchased by many slum-dwellers who have stolen electricity from the grid. So why is it that the poor will buy a television, but not the electricity needed to run it? Why will they pay for a cell phone before they can charge it up at home?

We in the West assume that the poor want easy energy like we have—and that all we need to do is figure out how to bring it to them cheaply. In reality, the more we investigated the commonly cited obstacles to distributed generation, the more we saw that product after product in the developing world faced similar problems—and overcame them. As we looked more closely, we realized that the core problem for distributed energy might not actually be a problem of supply—but of demand. And that is the topic we turn to next.

"The best form of marketing is to show people how solar works. So they can see that it's charging their mobile; they can see the TV's switched on. Then they really feel solar works!"

—Gildo Ongom, SolarNow retailer, Moroto, Uganda

Energy Generation
Requires Demand Generation:

ADDRESSING AN OVERLOOKED NEED

"A consumer market is nothing less than a lifestyle built around a product," as Erik Simanis, a senior researcher at the Center for Sustainable Global Enterprise at Cornell University, wrote in a 2009 *Wall Street Journal* article.[97] He was describing the difficulties that companies have getting people at the "Base of the Pyramid" to pay for new products. Simanis argued that it doesn't matter how great the product is—or even how affordable—if the consumer cannot clearly and easily see a reason for it within the construct of their daily lives. As capitalists have touted for decades, a market must start by creating need, even for something as seemingly essential as energy.

In other words: Success in the marketplaces of the developing world—just like in the developed world—is less about having the best product than it is about creating the demand for that product. That might seem obvious when you are selling something frivolous—a new soda, or a new shade of lipstick. But it is just as important when selling something that we see as vital, but others have lived without for, well, forever! The need to create demand needs to be placed at the heart of the solution to bringing energy to the developing world.

Before we zero in on delivering energy, it might be helpful to look at examples outside of the energy realm for some lessons learned. In 1999, Proctor & Gamble tried to market another product that would appear vital to the developing world: cheap and easy-to-use water-purification tablets.[98] The effort failed. That case provides an insightful example of the importance of helping customers see the benefit of changing their behaviors and/or beliefs and doing something in a different way. Let's look at it in more depth.

Like energy, the importance of clean drinking water is taken as a given in the developed world. Dirty water causes disease, and since we need water to survive, clean water is a matter of life or death. Yet clean water is scarce in the developing world, where more children die on a yearly basis from diarrhea caused by contaminated drinking water than from HIV/AIDS and malaria combined.[99] So, from the developed world's perspective, it was obvious that the developing world needed a solution to provide available clean drinking water.

Thus, when P&G developed its PUR water-purification product that could simply and cheaply purify even the most putrid water, it felt certain that it had created a product that would quickly find its way into every household in the

developing world. The purification tablets had been developed after extensive consumer research, including interviews
with potential users in the developing world. Taking a lesson
from Unilever's successful introduction of shampoo to poor
markets, P&G packaged its PUR product in cheap, single-
use sachets that cost just ten cents each. It was shelf-stable,
easy-to-use, and a single packet could purify three gallons of
water. And it worked—an assurance backed by P&G's partner in the effort, the U.S. Centers for Disease Control and
Prevention. According to market research, it should have
been a tremendous success. Instead, from a profitability perspective, it was a colossal failure.[100]

The main reason PUR packets failed was simple: People
didn't buy them. But why not? Wasn't clean water an essential need? Was ten cents too high a price to pay to keep
one's children healthy? Not necessarily. But for many people
in the developing world, water was something that was
free.[101] Suddenly, three gallons would cost ten cents. And
P&G hadn't rolled out an advertising campaign to explain
why they should change their behavior and buy something
that, on the face of it, didn't appear to alter a commodity
that usually cost nothing. Just as bottled water was a bou-
tique product for decades until marketers convinced the
West that it was worth paying for, the developing world
market was not ready to buy something they saw as theirs
by right.[102] In short, it didn't matter how good the product
was, how supposedly deep the need it was designed to fulfill,
or how applicable the business model. If a marketplace for
a product doesn't already exist, the product will not sell.
And for a market to exist, people have to be conditioned or

educated to the point where they demanded the product in the first place. In the case of clean water, they most likely first needed to be educated about the dangers of their current water supply. Given that people had lived with free, albeit contaminated water for their entire lifetimes—as well as those of their parents', and parents' parents—this is not necessarily the easiest sale—especially when competing for scarce discretionary dollars.

Seth Godin, writing in the magazine *Fast Company*, a publication focused on entrepreneurship and innovation, argues roughly the same thing in his article "Marketing at the Base of the Pyramid." According to Godin, it doesn't matter how great a particular product is, how well it's packaged, or how well it's sold, companies cannot and should not expect to simply put something in front of a person in the developing world and expect them to buy it.[103] Before people with a tiny amount of discretionary income will purchase a new product, they've got to believe that it will undoubtedly benefit their lives. To get to that point, anyone interested in bringing a product to market in the developing world has to first make people aware of the product and its benefits and then give them a reason to demand to have it.

So the first lesson is the importance of advertising: a reality almost always overlooked by social-sector organizations and governments, and even neglected, in PUR's case, by the multinational business Proctor & Gamble. Understanding the need to market a product that seems as if it should sell itself is the first step toward success in the developing world. The second step is marketing successfully. Marketing, advertising, and product-awareness efforts that work in the developed world often do not do the trick in the developing world. For one thing, developing world consumers are simply harder to reach. For companies accustomed to touching their customers through modern mediums such as television, it's sobering to note that in India, perhaps the largest bottom-of-the-pyramid market, only 41% of the population has access to a TV.[104] Since customer adoption starts with customers learning about the product itself, companies have to be nimble enough to tailor their advertising to a market not fully penetrated by mass media. For instance, in its attempts to market Breeze 2 in 1, a soap that also doubled as a shampoo, Hindustan Unilever hired street performers—magicians, singers, dancers, and actors—to tailor their performances to include references to and product information about the Breeze 2 in 1 product. The result was an 8% increase in awareness of Breeze 2 in 1 within the specific region of Northern India where the awareness campaign was carried out.[105] While not as creative as hiring street performers, Smart Communications, a mobile-telecommunications company in the Philippines, found success in buying advertising space on jeepneys, a predominant form of public transportation in the Philippines, as well as on the sides of ubiquitous three-wheeled taxis.[106]

Advertising must reach potential customers in ways that are already integrated into the patterns of their particular lives. When this is done well, the results can be spectacular. Grameen Shakti, a successful solar retailer in Bangladesh that is discussed in detail in the next chapter, created demand by involving local teachers and elected leaders to educate rural people about the benefits of electricity.[107] By enlisting high-status leaders in villages, and teachers who not only held status but naturally spoke to large numbers of villagers, they created a cheap viral marketing campaign that tied the status of villagers to the status of their own products.

Making sure that potential customers know that the product exists is crucial—but it is just one step. Next, consumers must understand what a product does—*and how that product can benefit them.* Connecting those dots is not obvious. Consider the case of mobile banking.

Safaricom, a mobile-phone company, has become famous for its system of allowing customers in Africa to transfer money via their phones. With the slogan, "Send Money Home," their system (named M-PESA) used advertising to directly explain how its product served a need that Safaricom believed already existed within Kenyan communities.[108] People in Kenya were already transferring money from cities where they worked to home villages where their families lived, often by carrying or sending a friend to carry a sum over long distances. But this method was often slow, and prone to theft, violence, and other ills.[109] Kenyans caught on quickly to the benefits of transferring money in a new way that avoided these ills. In a short amount of time, a marketplace, largely engineered by the awareness efforts of Safaricom, was created around the need to get money from one place to another in a nation without a pervasive banking structure.

More interesting for us, however, was that the uptake for the M-PESA service wasn't nearly as fast in neighboring Tanzania.[110] While M-PESA had 2.7 million users 14 months after its launch in Kenya, it had one-tenth as many—just 280,000—14 months after starting in Tanzania.[111] The reason for the slow uptake wasn't that the average Tanzanian wasn't familiar with the M-PESA brand itself (product awareness), but rather that while the average Tanzanian knew about the brand, they had much lower financial awareness, and didn't understand what the product actually *did for them.* Banking rates in Tanzania are about half what they are in Kenya— more than half of the population is unaware of debit cards or ATM machines.[112] In other words, customers in Kenya often used financial services, and just had to be convinced that M-PESA was a better way to make transactions. Customers in Tanzania had to be educated about the use of financial services in the first place![113] Advertising required not just brand awareness, but education about what the product could do for the average Tanzanian.

The challenge of bringing renewable energy to places like Kenya and Tanzania is to make sure that the products themselves don't follow the path of P&G's PUR water-treatment sachets, but rather spur the creation of an energy marketplace that self-perpetuates. Demand is an essential, overlooked part of that equation. Equally central, of course, is making sure consumers can buy the product you are selling. Pulling off that magic trick requires a focus on business models that work in the developing world, the topic of our next chapter.

"We convinced them that if we changed our attitudes, unlearned our perceptions, and opened ourselves to learning how our customers lived and worked, we could build a whole new business model and carve out a market where it was thought there was no business for us."

— Hector Ureta, director for new-market development, Cemex Corporation

Build a New Business Model
to Create a New Business

For most of history, those living in the slums of Mumbai or the huts of rural Africa were seen as charity cases. At worst, they were ignored; at best, they were recipients of outside largesse. The one thing they were not, were customers. At income levels ranging from one to twenty dollars a day, the individual purchasing power of the poor was just not something that interested companies.

Traditional thinking, however, missed the larger point: In developing countries, the bulk of the buying power isn't in the hands of the minority rich, it is in the hands of the majority poor. For instance, Brazil's poorest citizens comprise almost 25 million households with a combined total annual income of $73 billion.[114] If you take the largest 18 emerging economies and add up all the households with annual incomes under $6,000, the result is 680 million households with a total annual income of $1.7 trillion—a number that is roughly equivalent to Germany's annual GDP.[115] This is real money and a lot of it. The poor in the developing world may be poor on an individual basis, but their collective purchasing power is massive.

Meanwhile, those who have worked in the slums of Mumbai know that the poor are not as bereft of material goods as many might think. Many are simply locked in a system where the big-ticket items like a home are out of reach. So these individuals engage in buying smaller items such as TVs and gas stoves. For instance, in the Mumbai shantytown of Dharavi, a warren of tin roofs and burlap-bag walls, 85% of the households own a television set, 75% own a pressure cooker, and 56% own a gas stove.[116] Buying a home may never be a possibility, but these slum dwellers are a real market for items that directly improve their lives immediately. With 680 million households like this out there, that's a lot of collective purchasing power.

So if the poor have money to spend, our question becomes a query more common in the ad agencies of Madison Avenue than in the offices of the World Bank. How do you sell to the poor—and more specifically, how do you sell them energy?

To answer that question, we must first turn to shampoo and cell phones, areas where innovative companies and smart individuals have figured out how to create new purchasing models that tap into the buying patterns of the poor. By solving some of the financial obstacles we described in Chapter Two, these companies have found the collective purchasing power at the base of the pyramid to be staggeringly high.[117]

We identify three business-model innovations that meet the financial realities of selling to the poor. The first divides the product into units that are affordable within the reality of the paycheck cycle for the world's low-income families. The second relies on collective financing, such as through family ownership or a rental system that collectivizes ownership costs in the way that Zipcar now does in the United States—issues we touched on in Chapter Two. The third model focuses on turning a product from an expense into an asset by transforming it into an income-producing or cost-saving device. All offer learning points, and we will discuss each in turn.

MATCHING THE PRODUCT TO THE PAYCHECK: DESIGNING OR PACKAGING FOR AFFORDABILITY

Most products have been designed and manufactured for the developed world. As a result, poor consumers are rarely offered products that are designed with the economic realities of their lives in mind. Take for instance a bottle of shampoo.

Buying shampoo in the developed world is an afterthought—something thrown into your shopping cart as you stroll down the supermarket aisle. A low-end bottle might cost three bucks. But in the world of the poor, where the daily income may be only a dollar or two a day, a three-dollar bottle of shampoo is an extravagance—the equivalent of a $400 pair of shoes for an office worker making $50,000 a year!

So few poor people are going to buy shampoo. Assuming, of course, that companies insist on selling shampoo in the same-sized packaging that they would sell it for in a developed world market. Smart companies astutely realized that it's better to match the packaging to the customer's current purchasing power rather than to wait around for the customer's purchasing power to match the packaging.

In India, large companies such as Hindustan Lever (a subsidiary of Unilever) and Proctor & Gamble sell the majority of their shampoo in single-use packets.[118] Just a few years after hitting on this new packaging, 95% of all shampoo products currently sold in India are sold in single-use packets—and many don't even require water, thus making them even more attractive to those living in poverty.[119]

This model of matching the product's price to the sums available to the consumer is not limited to personal care products or household goods—sometimes it can even be applied to the house itself. Take for instance the *Patriomonio Hoy* Project that began in 1998 in Mexico's rural villages and urban slums. *Patriomonio Hoy*, roughly translated as "Personal Property Today," evolved out of the frustration by Cemex Corporation, one of the world's largest cement and building materials companies, at its inability to tap into the low-income market. The leadership of Cemex knew that the potential market numbered in the millions and that low-income families were already constructing shelters and homes. But their homes were built slowly, laboriously, and from materials that created no profit for Cemex.

The economic communities that Cemex began looking at were roughly similar to many of the other communities that we have already mentioned. According to the UN, roughly half of Mexico's population of 110 million lives on less than $2 a day. An estimated 30% of its workforce is "informal," meaning that their income tends to be off the books, and they pay no taxes—such as the roadside entrepreneur who sells flowers or snacks to those stuck in traffic.[120] But whether living on $2 a day or perhaps having a slightly higher informal income, poor Mexicans, like the poor Indians in the Mumbai slums mentioned before, are still buying things. Many were buying building materials. What got Cemex's attention was that this low-income demographic kept buying mud bricks, iron rebar, and cinder blocks even during the depths of the downturn in the Mexican economy during the 1990s.[121] The problem for Cemex was that this obviously vibrant and resilient market wasn't buying *its* cement or its building supplies!

Much like Unilever and Proctor & Gamble's repackaging of their shampoo products to match the purchasing habits of their potential customers, Cemex set about trying to unearth ways in which it could better match its product and sales patterns to the buying cycles of this potentially new customer base. The program, *Patriomonio Hoy,* was developed after a team of Cemex employees conducted what amounted to an anthropological study of the building patterns of low-income Mexican households. The team discovered that while people did consistently build new homes, the timelines for these homes were often elongated and uncertain given the exposure of this economic demographic to sudden price hikes, supply shortages, and periods of unemployment.[122] They built their homes room by room, rather than all at once, leaving rooms unfinished when money was tight, and doing the construction work themselves.

Cemex targeted those areas of risk exposure and developed a business model that instilled certainty throughout the whole construction process—certainty for the buyers of materials as well as for Cemex. The *Patriomonio Hoy* program essentially consisted of a would-be homebuilder paying Cemex roughly $14 per week for just under a year and a half. This roughly $1,000 dollars purchased scheduled deliveries of building materials, and an added perk: consultations by Cemex staff architects. Cemex packaged all the necessary building materials together, like a do-it-yourself kit, making it easier on the homeowner/builder. And due to its substantial purchasing power, Cemex was able to keep the prices low and stable throughout the life of the project.[123] Cemex tapped a huge new market, turning a demographic that had been seen as undesirable and unprofitable into a steady source of revenue. Meanwhile, by 2005, *Patriomonio Hoy* aided the construction of 10,000 homes that were built faster and better than what had been built under the traditional, old methods.[124] *Patriomonio Hoy* is yet another example of where innovation and creative thinking can spawn a symbiotic relationship between private business and the world's poor and improve peoples' lives in the process.

Proctor & Gamble's shampoo in India and Cemex's *Patriomonio Hoy* in Mexico succeeded because they stopped trying to push the square peg of their traditionally packaged product through the round hole of the developing world consumer. Instead, they took their basic products and created methods to deliver them that met the needs of poorer consumers. In both situations, affordability was key—and in both cases, it was accomplished by divvying up the standard-sized product into smaller, more affordable units. Standard packaging made shampoo unaffordable; repackaging made it affordable. Standard ways of purchasing Cemex cement were unaffordable; *Patriomonio Hoy* made it affordable—and easier to use for what the poor were trying to do. Distributed renewable energy has traditionally faced the same problem: Photovoltaic, wind, and other methods have been too costly for poor consumers to purchase.

New thinking and packaging is part of a solution set which can be classified under the umbrella of "designing for extreme affordability." In each of these cases, the business should *begin* with the price a consumer might be willing to spend on an item, and design the product to fit the price—whether that requires bringing down the costs of raw materials, or packaging finished materials into smaller units.

Distributed energy purveyors are beginning to learn this lesson. The Grameen family of nonprofits, under the leadership of Muhammad Yunus, has begun to transform the business model of the energy sector, as Yunus did with micro-finance. Grameen's engineering teams partnered with a number of manufacturing firms to create a low-cost solar home system. Their product pairs a photovoltaic panel with a battery to store electricity, a charge controller that regulates the charging and discharging of the battery, fluorescent tube lights, connecting devices that allow users to charge a cell phone, television, and a number of other common devices, and installation kits. They managed to get the cost down to about $400 for their 50-watt system, the most popular size for their customers. This cost should continue to come down as the cost of photovoltaics drops: Mass-market production in China has already started to reduce costs by leaps and bounds.[125] Though prices saw a short-term increase due to silicon shortages thanks to a sudden spike in demand, industry experts suggest that over time, trendlines point toward continued cost reductions.[126]

But while Grameen had managed to reduce costs, it did not design for extreme affordability—it did not start with the price point consumers could pay, it started with the cheapest product they could make. Thus, they needed financing. Thanks to the relationship between their nonprofit and financial-sector sides, they could offer it. Through Grameen Bank, their parent company that pioneered micro-finance, they then offered financing—a customer can pay as little as 10% up front, and the rest in monthly installments with a 4% to 6% service charge.[127] With no subsidies, they now had a product that was desired and affordable to a significant segment of poor Bangladeshis. Grameen credits their long-term financing innovation as a key factor in their successful business model.[128]

Grameen Shakti's innovations in product and business models won them an Ashdown Prize and allowed them to provide power to more than 135,000 homes by 2008—with 5,000 homes being added each month. However, for the poorest of the poor, even these up-front costs are too much.

Saving more than $40 for the purchase and installation of a kit is a hardship for those supporting families on less than $400 a year. Luckily, there are other products that have swept developing markets despite such up-front costs. No product epitomizes such explosive growth quite like the cell phone.

CELL PHONES AND ZIPCARS: GROUP OWNERSHIP AND RENTAL MODELS

Cell phones are everywhere. Whether you are in Denver or Durban, Miami or Mumbai, they are ubiquitous. Even in the middle of war-torn Kabul or Baghdad, you can see person after person on their mobile phones. In the 1990s, less than 1% of the entire population of sub-Saharan Africa had a mobile phone subscription. By 2006, there were more than 110 million mobile subscribers, representing 17% of the total population of sub-Saharan Africa.[129] Mobile phone networks have made dinosaurs out of existing traditional telecommunication infrastructures and have stopped new infrastructure projects dead in their tracks.

What can distributed energy learn from cell phones? To understand the important lessons around the mobile phone in order to apply it to energy, it helps to look first at how cell-phone business models work in the developed world, and from there trace the subsequent ripple effects that have created waves across a host of different industries ranging from farming to banking.

When cell-phone companies entered the developing world, they first made the same leap that Proctor & Gamble,

Cemex, and Grameen Shakti did—they figured out how to package their products in ways that customers could afford. Instead of costly monthly plans that required a credit history, prepaid phone cards were introduced so that customers could purchase only the minutes needed, while companies could ensure income in a way that free phones with multiyear contracts couldn't provide.[130] Customers could buy cheaper texting options, or simply ring each other without picking up the receiver to transmit prearranged messages and save further on their monthly bills.

But the cost of the handset was still formidable—an average mobile phone without a prepaid plan cost somewhere between $60 to $90 in countries from India to Kenya, with the cheapest entry-level phone built in India by a local producer running about $20.[131] Yet even at that low price, the cost of a handset is a significant barrier to entry: A $20 phone for someone earning a dollar a day is equivalent to a $2,500 purchase made by someone earning $50,000 a year.

In fact, while the cell-phone revolution makes cell phones appear ubiquitous in the developing world, that's not precisely the case. To meet the relatively high up-front cost, many phones are collectively owned. Throughout the developing world, a family or extended family will pool together to buy and share one phone—an idea that we will investigate for energy in the next chapter. The multitude of families employing such a financing scheme led companies such as Nokia to develop multiple-user phonebooks, so that many different users could keep their contact lists private and separate on the same handset.[132] Grameen Shakti is experimenting with such an extended family–based model of electricity generation with bio-gas plants it has created that use cow dung and poultry waste to create electricity.[133] Crucially, these goods are not owned by "no one"—they are owned within a family circle that enforces joint responsibility for maintenance and upkeep.

But before such family-owned phones, the origin of the cell phone within the context of the developing market came about in perhaps the rawest form of capitalism imaginable: An enterprising individual with just enough capital to buy a phone purchased one, and then charged those around him to use it. This originally started with landline phones, but with the introduction of mobile-phone technologies the model quickly leapt to cell phones. Many small micro-finance initiatives saw this occurring and set about trying to assist. For instance, one of the world's best-known micro-finance institutions, Grameen Bank, created a program, dubbed Grameen Phone, which allowed women in Bangladesh to purchase a phone kit with an extra long-life battery for about USD $150 and then, essentially, create a business from renting out the airtime.[134] By 2006, this model was providing coverage to more than 28,000 villages and to more than 50 million individuals.[135] Grameen Phone is now Bangladesh's largest telecom provider.[136] And it has partnered with Grameen Shakti, which enables these village phone centers to power their phones with distributed generation![137] Similar programs have arisen in countries from Cameroon to Uganda. For one or two people per village, the phone itself became a business, as a sewing machine is for a tailor, or a rickshaw is for a rickshaw driver. But most people didn't try to own a phone. They bought a few minutes of call time, as needed.

In the developed world, some of the fastest-growing businesses are based on a mix of such "rental" or "service delivery" models for goods that were previously simply purchased outright. For instance, in dense urban areas, Zipcars are growing at a rapid pace. City owners are willing to trade the convenience of individual ownership to escape the hassle and expense of parking, taxes, and upkeep—as long as they can be assured of a car that is clean, functioning, relatively nearby, and available.

A related rental model—perhaps best termed "service delivery"—has also been adapted by the energy field in some cases. In Cambodia, electricity entrepreneurs run approximately 1,000 diesel-based power stations at which people can charge up batteries, and about 600 micro-grids that each provide power to several homes.[138] As with the village phone centers, many of these enterprises are simply a guy with a diesel generator or two and the know-how to connect these to provide electricity for products and homes. Many of them have also diversified their business model away from household use alone—an insight we will return to in the next section. They offer some services to small businesses that use power during the day when households do not. This market segmentation is important to ensure the functioning of their business and is rarely investigated by nonprofits trying to provide power to households alone. These entrepreneurs may be serving up to 75%–85% of the population with their energy—albeit not in a renewable form.[139] Most operate without financing and without formal licenses, charging relatively high prices—and yet, they have found a significant market because of significant demand.

Could a similar system work with distributed *renewable* energy? In fact, it is working—and not only in the developing world. Solar panels are also a major cost in the United States, a cost that industry leaders have worked to get around through smart business models and financing arrangements. For instance, Sun Edison and other industry leaders often choose to own the solar panels themselves, rent roofspace or land, and sell the electricity itself, rather than the panels, to the consumer. To date, commercial businesses have been the biggest players, reducing transaction costs for Sun Edison. In the U.S., these schemes often require feed-in tariff regulations that allow companies to make money by selling energy back to the grid. But they are also being used in the developing world in places where the grid does not exist. For instance, we already mentioned Fabio Rosa and his nonprofit and for-profit companies, respectively: IDEAAS and STA, which rent photovoltaic cells with an installation fee and a flat monthly fee. As with Zipcars, the company owns the product, and rents it out by time-units to the consumer, allowing up-front costs to be lowered, and monthly costs to be kept to low monthly rates. The technology has caught on so quickly that it has created a healthy competition with the centralized grid, which Brazil's central government is now extending.[140] Where the solar kits are renting well, the central power company has promised to extend the grid in order to prove its own worth—and meet its legal mandates to provide power to the poor—a form of competition that reduces profit for IDEAAS and STA, but ultimately helps the poor.[141]

In another form of this collective ownership or rental model, Grameen Shakti has created a Micro-Utility System that allows an entrepreneur to purchase a system and share some of the electrical capacity with neighbors. The entrepreneur is responsible for payments to Grameen, and makes up some of that cost by selling energy at a slightly higher price to users of the system. More than 10,000 such systems are operating in Bangladesh.[142]

The micro-utility model points to the next, and most important, innovation we found. Collective use helped the cell phone get a toehold in the developing world. But in and of itself, it was not enough to create a product that sold like wildfire. The most important lesson for financing cell phones was not simply making the cost per unit cheaper—it was looking to the income, rather than the expense, side of the ledger.

YOU CAN'T AFFORD NOT TO OWN ONE

A rickshaw creates one job: for the driver. A sewing machine does the same for the tailor. And a cell phone originally did the same for the owner of the village phone center, just as Grameen's Micro-Utility is doing for the owner of the energy source. But what is exciting about mobile phones in the developing world is not where they started, but where they went from there. Rather than an end in themselves, they became a foundational technology that enabled other businesses to expand, and more wealth to be created. This is the third insight in selling to the poor: Focus on income-producing technologies, and on marketing them for income-producing uses.[143]

As cell phones became more common, services proliferated to use them in new and innovative ways. Many of these services created ways to save costs and make money. Soon, owners of cell phones were paying off their initial investments within a matter of months—and then making profits they had never seen before. Cell-phone ownership moved from a collective to a private good because of a third innovation: turning the good from an expense into an income-producing asset.

With an income possibility from cell phones, they could become sensible targets for lending. Asia has plentiful micro-credit. Much of Africa has a history of lending circles where each member pays an amount in, and then one gets to take the entire pot, use it to generate income, and then return the original funds borrowed to the group again at a set time, whereupon the pot moves to another member of the circle. It was the income-producing nature of cell phones that allowed them to be purchased through micro-finance and lending circles—because the purchaser could count on new income produced by the phone to allow her to pay back the original cost of the handset.

For instance, developing-country fishermen are using their phones to determine the best places with the highest prices to take their catch. Farmers are using phones to send text messages to adjacent villages and towns to check market prices for agricultural goods, creating more standardized prices across regions and providing more profit to the rural poor. Not only do such calls give them a chance to increase their gross margins, it eliminates the previous transportation costs associated with traveling to various markets in order to ascertain the best price.[144] Studies by the consulting firm

McKinsey & Co. suggest that raising wireless penetration by 10% can lead to a .5% increase in GDP—serious numbers with national ramifications.

Mobile banking is another cost-saver enabled by the cell phone, the marketing of which we discussed in the last chapter. In the developed world, banking institutions and individual bank accounts are prevalent. But in the developing world, large swaths of the population live without the security and convenience of a bank. They have no ability to earn interest or save a regular piece of their paycheck each month. Meanwhile, they pay large fees to cash checks or transfer money—considerable expenses in economies where an extended family has one wage earner who often leaves home and works far away, sending small savings back home on a regular basis.[145] Safaricom has now brought the convenience and savings of banking to the 80% of Kenyans who don't have a bank account, thanks to the M-PESA program that allows users to send small amounts of money via SMS text messaging. M-PESA agents, including airtime dealers, petrol stations, and supermarkets, act as mini-banks, allowing Safaricom customers to deposit and withdraw funds directly from them. Funds deposited with M-PESA agents are then available to transfer to other Safaricom customers via text.[146] The use of cell phones to locate the most fruitful markets or to serve as mobile banks, represents innovation that occurred internal to the developing world. While Western companies and social-sector organizations have subsequently tried to improve and expand on these innovations, the most fascinating thing about cell phones is that they formed a foundational technology upon which the developing world built business methods that created wealth. It's not having a cell phone that is exciting: It's what the individuals do with that technology that matters. Mobile phones provided the key to opening the door to latent creativity within the developing world. This ability to use the mobile phone to innovate beyond the traditional bounds of telecommunication and into realms where the phone is both an income-generating and cost-saving device is what is truly driving the adoption of mobile phones throughout the world.

Energy is, of course, perhaps the most basic foundational technology. Even businesses that don't traditionally need electricity—such as a barbershop—can stay open longer, gaining additional income and competitive advantage. Other businesses can reap efficiency rewards by employing computers, refrigeration to keep perishable inventory from spoiling, and other devices that increase business turnover, such as moving from manual to electric sewing machines. Finally, as Grameen Shakti's CEO has stated, electricity opens up myriad new business opportunities—from TV halls and computer training centers to mobile-phone charging stations.[147]

One reason that starting a market through sales to income-producing entities makes sense, is that it yields demonstration effects that further drive a market by encouraging others to buy the technology. For instance, d.light is a company that combines LED lights, solar panels, and proprietary energy-management tools to create a solar lamp desired by the developing world. The lamps sell for about $25, but those who bought them found that they paid for themselves by allowing consumers to work later into the night and increase their income. As co-founder Nedjip Tozun explained: "Two families in a village of 47 families in India took the risk of buying the lights instead of their former kerosene lamps. The quality of the light was so much better that 'All of a sudden, the two families were able to work at night . . . their average monthly income increased from $12 to $18, and they could save the time [they would otherwise have spent] traveling to buy more kerosene.' Within a few days, the entire village had sprung for the lights."[148]

In a nice case of one foundational technology creating markets for another, cell phones may be playing their own role in the creation of a market for distributed energy. One of the curbs on cell-phone growth is reliable energy to power them—making cell-phone owners a significant customer base for electricity entrepreneurs with diesel generators in countries from Cambodia to Ghana. Lack of reliable energy is such a significant barrier to further cell-phone penetration that Motorola is actually offering solar-based powering stations to entrepreneurs in Uganda, and is testing wind-and-solar–based base stations in Namibia.[149]

An innovative startup is already taking advantage of the demand created by the spread of cell phones. Fenix International is the company behind the ReadySet—an elegant little self-contained device holding a battery that can charge anything powered by a USB or able to plug into a cigarette lighter. The tough unit weighs less than ten pounds and requires little maintenance and no know-how: It's simply plug and play. To supply the energy, the ReadySet can clamp onto a car battery—but Fenix also created a series of renewable energy plug-in modules, ranging from a rugged, small solar panel to wind and micro-hydro, to a gadget you can attach to any bicycle so that pedal power can charge up the battery. Meanwhile, a range of applications on the output side lets the ReadySet charge anything from a few mobile phones at a time to an electric light or refrigerator—and the platform is open, allowing anyone to develop new "apps" to either generate electricity or to use that energy.

The ReadySet retails for just $150, along with the cost of additional add-ons to generate the electricity itself. But their most important innovation is probably their business model, which draws on all the lessons we've discussed here. They started by realizing that their product needed to be income-generating for the end user. That led them to look for a new market niche—one they found by selling to cell-phone companies. They noticed that some of the hottest businesses around the energy-poor world, with the largest distribution systems, were cell-phone companies. But while millions of people own cell phones, they often had to walk days to get their phones charged, and then they subsequently conserved their minutes jealously. They were also a market—many charged their phones via entrepreneurs who had jury-rigged car batteries in ways that worked, but were dangerous and environmentally problematic—and charged 25 cents a charge—real money, if scaled.

Fenix International did the field research and economic modeling in sub-Saharan Africa to show the cell-phone companies that if their customers could keep their phones charged more regularly, the companies would gain more revenue.

After all, only a charged phone can send texts, make calls, or be used for anything at all! By showing the market potential being lost to uncharged phones, Fenix International was able to sell the companies on a mutually beneficial business partnership. The cell-phone companies themselves would purchase the ReadySets—then resell them with a slight markup to their cell-phone sales force. These distribution kiosks could then either resell ReadySets to customers—or become energy hubs themselves, adding the ability to charge electronic devices to their realm of products for sale in kiosks across the country. The demonstration effect of the ReadySet in these cell-phone kiosks helps generate demand in other businesses—demand that Fenix International further pumps by explicitly marketing the ReadySet as an income generator, with financial models that demonstrate how the system can pay for itself in as little as three months. Meanwhile, by partnering with the cell-phone companies, Fenix International creates a guaranteed market for its product that has allowed it to raise startup capital on the private market, and operate as a for-profit company. Their first ReadySets should hit Uganda by the time this book has gone to print.

Startups are always risky ventures. Like Grameen and Safaricom, Fenix International has all the ingredients for a successful startup: visionary and business-savvy leadership, a great product, and a smart business model. By building an affordable technology, finding a means to cut costs still further through a business partnership, ensuring demand-generating demonstrations, and marketing their product as an income-producing appliance, ReadySet has done all that it can to ensure success. But for a market to exist, it needs more than smart businesses and good products. It needs an environment that ensures that all the obstacles cited in Chapter Two can be overcome—from demand generation to human capital, government policy to financing. What that environment looks like in practice is the topic of our next chapter.

"We want to design things so that a farmer can decide to leave his farm and support his family selling water pumps or drip-irrigation tubing. We want things to be sold at a price that covers the cost of manufacturing and distribution."

— James Patell, Stanford professor who co-teaches the "Entrepreneurial Design for Extreme Affordability" course[150]

Shaping the Ecosystem:
Creating a Market Friendly Environment

One of the first interviews we conducted upon embarking on this project was with the executive director of a terrific, established nonprofit that focused on bringing solar power to villages and townships throughout the developing world. This organization produced fantastic results in the areas in which they've been able to operate. Their products are of first-rate quality, their installers are highly skilled, and the panels are affordable because, well, they're donated by this organization and therefore free. This nonprofit represents the best full-service, A–Z aid model out there. It has changed the lives of people in the villages in which it works. But sadly, it hasn't changed the world.

We are hardly faulting that organization. Like most nonprofits, it relies heavily on the efforts of a tiny group of dedicated individuals raising funds for a particular project site and then delivering on that site. It's simply that the world is huge, the problem of energy poverty just as large, and any all-in-one, single-entity solution simply cannot scale to the requisite size to adequately address the worldwide situation. In short, this basic aid donation model has largely failed over the last thirty years to scale enough to bring energy to the entire developing world. We believe it will continue to fail for the next thirty years if left unchanged.

Scaling energy cannot be done with charity—it can only be accomplished via a dynamic market for energy in the developing world. Such a market depends on entrepreneurial businesses, but is buoyed by reduced and reformed government regulation, competent human capital, and financing. This chapter looks at these elements of market creation, bringing together the lessons drawn from the rest of this book.

AN ECOSYSTEM MODEL— LEVERAGING SOCIAL-SECTOR EXPERTISE TO BUILD MARKETS

With 70% of the population in sub-Saharan Africa lacking access to electricity, the energy situation can most adequately be described as abysmal. For the 90% of rural areas that are energy-impoverished, the situation is even more deplorable.[151] So, what can be done?

One solution is the A–Z, start-to-finish, donation-based aid model. Much like the one described above, a nonprofit organization can arrive on the scene, conduct a thorough analysis of the conditions, raise funds, secure supplies, and install a set of top-notch solar home systems throughout a particular village. This solution works—but only within the handful of villages lucky enough to be targeted by these nonprofits. How can this solution scale? Aside from armies of nonprofit workers laden with unlimited donations from deeply committed philanthropists, the short answer is that it can't.

The Rural Energy Foundation (REF) takes another approach. Based out of The Netherlands and operating across sub-Saharan Africa, REF eschews the model that uses donations to supply equipment procurement, construction, or installation. Instead, it focuses its efforts on creating a marketplace for energy (PV solar being its preferred generation technology) by essentially empowering already-existing PV retailers.

By the dawn of the 21st century, many retailers across Africa had already realized that harnessing power from the sun makes sense and, on that intuition, entered into the retail solar business. What REF discovered, however, was that while these early solar entrepreneurs grasped the promise of solar, they didn't have the requisite business skills or internal assets to persuade others to pay for this promise. Essentially, they couldn't generate enough demand for solar products to create viable, sustainable solar businesses. As such, REF's mission became targeted at helping solar retailers better run their businesses, with a particular focus on generating demand for their products.

The case of Moses Okesa is particularly representative. Prior to the arrival of REF, Okesa was a struggling solar retailer operating in the northern part of Uganda. Okesa went into the PV solar business because he thought it made sense for his area of Uganda given that the region was highly focused on local clan and tribe relations rather than on the central government, and people had no real experience (or desire) to pay bills to an entity outside the community.[152] However, Okesa and other like-minded retailers struggled because, in his words, they "didn't have capacity to advertise themselves, their programs, or the capacity for quality technical training."[153]

REF's solution to Okesa's dilemma was the introduction of the SolarNow program. This program is largely an educational one designed to provide technical and business support to Okesa and other existing solar dealers like him. REF also encourages additional retailers to move into the solar retail space by providing them with similar training as well as instruction on the benefits of solar energy and how those benefits could be translated into profits for those peddling them.[154]

One of the biggest needs that REF's SolarNow program seeks to fulfill is the need for market awareness, because, in the words of REF employee Chris Mulindwa, "so many people out here in the field don't know about solar."[155] The way REF and the SolarNow program do this isn't fancy or revolutionary. In fact, its simplicity is likely what makes it so effective. REF provides participants in the SolarNow program with portable demonstration kits that allow the retailers to show people how the systems work and, more importantly, how the systems can work for *them*.[156] Clearly demonstrating both the benefit of the product, as well as how the product fits into the buyer's life, makes a huge difference in uptake. It's hard to overemphasize the importance of demonstrating to people how owning a solar home system, or even a solar lantern, can benefit them.

REF designs the demonstration kits to focus primarily on demonstrating to people what they can do with a solar home system. Two of the demonstration kits are a bush barbershop kit and a mobile-phone charging kit. Each kit demonstrates what a solar system would enable a budding entrepreneur to do, versus what they are currently able to accomplish without one. A shopkeeper with a system can make additional money and draw more customers by offering people a place where they can charge their phones. A hairdresser can stay open longer than her competitors, thus earning additional revenue.

The fact that REF's demonstration model focuses on business uses, not homes, is no accident. As we've mentioned before, it behooves businesses to sell products to those most able to pay the upfront costs: small entrepreneurs who believe that the product will allow them to quickly pay off their initial investment. Meanwhile, selling to businesses generates ripple-effect demand that can create scale for more sales. Take for instance the fictional shopkeeper mentioned above. If the sun sets at 7:00 P.M., but she can now stay open till 10:00 P.M. because of the power provided to her by her PV system with battery storage, she essentially operates as a monopoly for 3 hours since her competitors without a PV system had to shut down come nightfall. While this is excellent for the shopkeeper, it is pretty problematic for her PV system–less competitors. While not a complete certainty, it is highly likely that those same competitors will soon have to find their way to a SolarNow dealer in order to compete with the original solar-powered shopkeeper. Over time, through these ripple effects, it will become the de facto state of shopkeeping in that particular area that if you want to survive as a business, you'll have to operate at night. To do so, you'll need to buy a solar electrical system. At this point, demand has created a self-sustaining market. By focusing on businesses, the internal dynamics of competition create even more demand—allowing adaptation to rapidly scale, and solar businesses to stay in business.

The above is a hypothetical scenario, but it is grounded in the same reality that expanded d.light's customer base from two families to the entire village in a matter of days after the solar lights helped such early adopters increase their monthly earnings by one-third. Nor are the business opportunities from electricity limited to longer business hours. In Mr. Okesa's village, the owner of a local bar used the energy generated from his solar home system to provide the power to run a refrigerator in which he could keep his beer cold.[157] The ability to provide cold beer makes his customers happy and gives the owner a significant competitive advantage over bars that are still selling warm beer. If other bar owners don't quickly get a fridge (and the PV system to go with it), they will soon find themselves with far fewer customers. Demand for cold beer creates demand for solar power.

The technical support and branding efforts provided by REF should not be underestimated, either—they are essential to overcoming the legacy of poor technology and maintenance that hold back a market. In order to participate in its four-day training course and receive permission to operate under the SolarNow brand, retailers must commit to providing high-quality installations and good after-sales service. Retailers are required to call customers at predetermined periods of time to ensure that the systems are still running and operating to standard.[158] This quality management ensures the creation and perpetuation of goodwill from people toward solar products—crucial when many of the poor are risk-averse, and when one poor-quality product that impoverishes its owner can set a new market back for years.

The results of the SolarNow program have been inspiring. There are now more than 200 SolarNow branded retailers operating in nine African countries, including Uganda, Tanzania, and Senegal.[159] To date, SolarNow branded retailers have sold 57,000 solar home systems and more than 36,000 solar lanterns.[160] REF has worked with micro-finance organizations to develop programs that help individuals pay for the system up front. Most systems repay that initial cost in savings on kerosene and batteries over the first one to three years of the system's life—a fairly short, easily foreseeable return on investment.[161] For its efforts, REF was the 2010 recipient of the prestigious Ashden Award for Sustainable Development for Africa, presented by the John Ellerman Foundation.

REF is a nonprofit that figured out its job was to sell a service, not a product. By helping the marketplace, REF accomplished its mission more efficiently and effectively. Another Ashden Award winner, Zara Solar Ltd., *is* the retailer. And in the words of its owner, Mohamedrafik Parpia, the goal of Zara Solar, at least originally, was not to make a positive impact on the community, but rather to make money.[162] In many respects, Parpia's Zara Solar is what the majority of REF's SolarNow branded retailers aspire to become.

Mr. Parpia and Zara Solar operate in a near-perfect environment for solar-generated distributed energy. Located in Mwanza, the second-largest city in Tanzania with a population of more than 3 million people, Zara Solar operates in a region where only 2% of rural households have reliable access to electricity.[163] Emerging out of an electronics business in 2001, Zara Solar is a stand-alone solar retailer. It represents the potent combination of local business acumen, private financial investment, and international development efforts that, when blended together, can create a market where businesses can thrive and renewable energy can scale.

Zara Solar's business model is quite simple. It sells solar home systems to those who live too far away from the grid to have access to power and to those who do not care to be dependent on the intermittent nature of the Tanzanian electrical system. It began by marketing to businesses and higher-end consumers, and most of its customers currently pay outright for the systems (which average about US$570). After becoming established, the company has recently started selling through Savings and Credit Co-Operative Societies that enable more variable payment plans and allow it to reach another market segment.[164]

Zara Solar has marketed its products in much the same way that REF encourages its SolarNow retailers to market theirs: by showing people how to make money from solar energy. One of the more novel success stories for Zara is the story of a bait-shop owner who used a solar energy system to aerate the water in his fishpond. He chose the solar system because his old, diesel generator kept breaking and too many of his fish were dying during the time it took to get it fixed. He says his new system is much more reliable.[165] His story is of particular note because it anecdotally disproves the notion that clean, renewable systems are less reliable than inefficient, diesel generators—a common misconception in many communities.

Zara Solar is a success story. But it did not succeed alone. It benefited from an ecosystem of organizations that each played a role in creating a market where small businesses could be successful. Zara Solar began from the base of a firm that already existed. To grow into the solar market, it needed a large infusion of cash. With a banking infrastructure not well-suited to helping small and medium-sized businesses, Mr. Parpia was lucky to be operating in a region serviced by a social enterprise organization that provide venture capital for the energy sector, E+Co. Zara did not need a tiny microloan of $100—it needed real capital to grow a real business. Luckily, E+Co is part of a new breed of hybrid nonprofit or low-profit social-business enterprises that exist to invest in developing world businesses and to help them grow and scale in ways that would otherwise not be possible—while perpetuating themselves by earning a small return on investment, with interest.[166] E+Co invested US$350,000 in Zara Solar spread out across three different loans.[167] This cash allowed Zara to buy in greater bulk and thus attain better pricing, purchase more quality inventory, and expand in other areas. Over the course of E+Co's investment, Zara Solar's sales have skyrocketed. From 2005 with sales of less than US$200,000 per year and negligible to negative net income, Zara has become profitable and, as of 2008, increased sales to US$1.6 million per year and generated a positive net income of US$250,000. E+Co's investment essentially helped the inventory-intensive Zara Solar bridge the "valley of death" that claims so many businesses as they struggle from founding to being profitable.[168]

The final piece in the success of Zara Solar is the role that the international development community played in Mwanza. One of the more interesting parts of Zara Solar's business model is how it handles installation. While its business relies on quality products and installation, Zara did not invest in the ability to do every installation itself. Instead, it refers a significant portion of its customers—especially those who live significant distances outside the city—to specially trained solar electricians. By identifying and contracting with an ever-expanding set of technicians, both numerically and geographically, Zara Solar has created a symbiotic relationship between the dealer and the installer. When Zara Solar makes a sale, they refer the purchaser to a technician based in their area, thus benefiting that technician. Conversely, when someone approaches the technician to inquire about solar products, the technician refers that person to Zara Solar, thus bringing more business to Zara.

Where did this network of competent, trained solar technicians come from? Enter the international development community. Beginning in 2004, the United Nations Development Programme (UNDP) in coordination with the Global Environment Fund (GEF) led a five-year effort entitled "Transformation of the Rural Photovoltaic Market in Tanzania." This effort was squarely targeted in the Mwanza region and focused on a wide range of activities—all of which were focused not on providing a product, but on easing the introduction of a market. With greater resources than REF, they could assist in market creation in a broader range of ways, overcoming a number of hurdles mentioned in Chapter One. And by focusing on creating a market, rather than on directly marketing solar, they beat their target numbers for PV systems sold by a factor of five.[169]

What did they do to ease the creation of a market? First, they focused on policy, an area hard for small businesses to tackle, and easier for major aid donors. They worked with the government to reduce import duties on solar technologies and components. They also helped the Tanzanian government create a Rural Energy Master Plan and made sure that PV was heavily featured in it.[170]

This effort was helped by a program that prominently supported and featured advertising campaigns designed to increase awareness among decisionmakers as well as consumers. This part of the campaign featured messaging targeted at potential end users through multiple channels from TV and radio to calendars, leaflets, and additional types of brochures.[171] It also developed a number of potential models for income-generating activities powered by solar PV as a method to spur interest. Again, they hit on the central component of selling energy technology: making it profitable to the end user.

Last but not least, the program trained more than 200 technicians from Mwanza and neighboring regions in sizing, installation, troubleshooting, and maintenance, creating a certification process for solar technicians. Additionally, the program assisted the Vocational Education and Training Authority (VETA) in introducing solar PV curricula and, additionally, trained 12 VETA instructors to lead follow-on training.[172]

It is in this favorable operating environment that Zara Solar was able to flourish. The greatest part of its success story, however, is not to be found in sales numbers or profit margins, but in the inherent scalability of the various activities that have produced a dynamic market for solar technologies in and around the city of Mwanza. Instead of one institution or individual doing everything, each entity—the entrepreneur, the social-sector investment firm, the government, and the international development organization—was mobilized to act in its area of greatest strength. The result was a synergistic environment that generated the demand for solar PV as well as a market to meet, grow, and sustain that demand over the long term.

COMPONENTS OF A SUCCESSFUL MARKET ENVIRONMENT

So what are the key components for a successful business environment? They are the same as the obstacles described in Chapter Three, only turned on their heads. By focusing on each sector's strengths, social-sector organizations, governments, and international businesses can each leverage their abilities to create a market friendly environment for developing country entrepreneurs. Here are the five elements of a successful strategy:

1) Create a Supportive Legal Environment, Including Deregulation and Low Tariffs

In the 1990s, assisted by international development banks, nonprofits, and bilateral aid programs providing technical assistance, country after country in Africa began deregulating their telecommunications markets. They abolished monopolies that had traditionally controlled the telephone sector. They privatized firms, and allowed new firms to compete. Instead of owning the telephone companies as public utilities, they created regulatory authorities to oversee the now-burgeoning sector.[173] These moves were the catalyst that allowed cell phones to take off and work their miraculous effects on the developing world.

Building a market in a highly regulated environment has to start with improvements to that regulation, so that distributed generation businesses can exist at all. A supportive legal and regulatory environment need not advantage distributed energy—but at the very least, it should not disadvantage the market. In countries with a weak rule of law, improved regulation can be essential to enable insurance against risk, hedging against expropriation, and other measures. Useful ideas include:

- Putting regulations in place that allow businesses to provide distributed generation. This may require ending monopolies on utility provision of energy, or restricting such monopolies to centralized generation rather than to all energy provision. It may also require the creation of regulatory authorities for the distributed generation (DG) space, though a light touch in terms of measures needed to start a DG company is preferable in order to reduce opportunities for corruption and nepotism;

- Ensuring low or no import duties or tariffs on distributed energy components;

- Eliminating or reducing subsidies on competing forms of energy, such as kerosene or diesel;

- Legally enforced means for loan collection, to enable payment plans;

- Creating written, publicly available, and realistic long-term government electrification plans, so that banks can properly assess the market for distributed generation.[174]

- Where there is a widespread but problematic centralized grid, writing regulations that allow consumers to obtain payments for feeding-in energy from their distributed systems into the grid. When these take the form of subsidized payments, they can help jumpstart a small business market; however, they need not be set above market rates to provide a valuable signaling device to banks and businesses.

The best way to prod and assist this process from outside the country's own political system is likely to be the prospect of membership in global entities that the government itself wants to join —such as the WTO, which could insist on improved energy regulation as one of the qualifications of membership. In most cases, however, such a "carrot" is not available as an external prod. In these cases, multilateral banks, intergovernmental organizations, and think tanks can play a role, as they have done with the telephone industry and other markets. These entities can provide the push and the intellectual wherewithal to help governments to overcome entrenched interests and to be realistic in their plans so that utopian dreams of centralized electrification do not inhibit the market. Social-sector advocacy groups within a country, if they exist, can also be helpful—and can be assisted in their organization and advocacy by organizations such as the Center for International Private Enterprise (CIPE). A group such as CIPE can also help groups that advocate for the poor see that distributed generation could bring larger, longer-term benefits than subsidies for fossil fuels, for instance, which they might otherwise be tempted to advocate to continue.

2) Assist with Access to Capital—But Resist Subsidies

Grameen Shakti's electrification of Bangladesh is a huge success story. Yet their business acumen rested on the shoulders of supportive financing. The World Bank supported the Government of Bangladesh's Infrastructure Development Company Ltd. (IDCOL) on its plan to install 50,000 solar home systems from 2003 to 2008. A crucial element for enabling this market-based system to scale and prosper, was IDCOL's decision not to directly implement this program itself, but instead to provide soft loans and technical assistance to private businesses. In just two years, three years ahead of schedule, the program met its goal—and Grameen Shakti had favorable financing which allowed it to install 65% of those systems, while other private businesses and social-sector organizations also gained the capital they needed to install the rest.[175]

As with government regulation, there is a spectrum of actions that can make financing more or less favorable. The more measures implemented, the easier it is to jumpstart a market. Useful measures include:

- Technical assistance to local financial institutions to help them price risk for distributed generation projects;[176]
- Risk-sharing with local financial institutions through joint loans from international and local banks;
- Risk-sharing through publicly backed guarantees or public co-investment;[177]
- Risk-sharing through the provision of political risk insurance and similar instruments to mitigate or spread risk;
- Directly offering financing through social enterprises seeking to make low-return loans to achieve social goals, such as E+Co;
- Government tax incentives and other measures that encourage financial institutions to provide soft loans and favorable financing to the sector;
- Legal solutions that allow off-take agreements, contracts in which a buyer promises to purchase a resource at a given price once produced, so that banks are assured of a market and are more ready to lend;
- Encouraging banks and/or micro-credit organizations to establish business lines that provide consumer-level financing and to assist with monthly payment collection.

Again, international banks, development agencies, and social-sector organizations (both for-profit and nonprofit) are the best agents to support these measures—at least initially. While such financing, in an ideal world, would be provided at market rates by banks and venture capitalists, the reality is that the sector is simply too new, and expected rates of return are too low, to compete in an international market against the future Googles, Facebooks, and other potential businesses in which capital can be invested. Programs that have tried to harness such purely private funding other than initial angel investment have generally failed.[178]

However, social enterprises, including banks, venture funds, private-equity investors, and nonprofit organizations that can wait for long payback periods and don't require a high return on their investments, can use their capital to directly finance developing-world businesses, or, even better, to leverage local financial institutions in this sphere. The World Bank's Small & Medium Enterprise Department, for example, provided loans of US$500,000 to US$1 million to financial and nonprofit intermediaries within countries to make loans or equity investments. Intermediaries received long-term, low interest rates for up to ten years at 2.5%.[179] In cases like this one, where global or multinational banks are involved in this market, it is best for them to create a local subsidiary with reduced reporting requirements and other paperwork. Otherwise, reporting requirements required for such loans, while common in the world of foundations making grants to dependent nonprofits, can be onerous to business markets and can slow down projects to the point where they are no longer profitable for the local entrepreneur. For social enterprises to actually assist the business sector, they must provide their local loans in a manner more like any normal local bank loan, rather than as a foundation grant.[180]

Over time, financing can move to joint social-sector/business ventures. For a historical example, just turn again to the cell-phone market. Between 1995 and 2005, after deregulation, private companies invested the lion's share of the $25 billion pumped into sub-Saharan Africa's telecommunications sector.[181] A number of these private investors first entered these markets in joint partnership with entities such as the World Bank, which provided a sense of security in their investments, and in some cases political-risk insurance.[182] In this way, the sector can move, over time, to a more purely private model as distributed generation gains a foothold and proves its profitability.

Finally, at the consumer end of the market, for-profit or nonprofit micro-credit organizations can play a role as a collection agency that enables businesses to run rental or installation-payment models while outsourcing some of the collection costs. Grameen Shakti was able to draw on its parent organization, Grameen Bank, to provide consumer financing.[183] But businesses without such unique ties to a bank would do well to establish partnerships with existing micro-credit or banking operations to allow similar synergies. Providing small credit lines to both sellers of distributed generation equipment and to entrepreneurs establishing themselves as installation, repair, and maintenance personnel would help these markets expand.[184]

On both sides of the ledger, donors and governments must resist the urge to subsidize products. While subsidizing technology may seem like a way to jumpstart the market, in fact it kills markets from developing. Who in their right mind would buy a product at full price, when they could get it more cheaply or even for free? While cheap or free products may help the small number of people who benefit directly, subsidies are inherently uneconomical, so they can never be broad-based enough to scale to an entire population. Meanwhile, subsidies for the initial equipment do not continue to cover maintenance. And when technology is not maintained, the carcasses of broken products deter future efforts.

Nothing kills a market faster than subsidies for products. Yet governments and donors continue to provide and install such technology across the country at subsidized rates in the hope of "doing good." Meanwhile, by destroying the market, they stop the ability of a technology to scale through market forces—hurting the poor they are trying to help.[185]

3) Help Develop Affordable Technology

It should come as no surprise that the poor are extremely price-sensitive. Bringing down the price of goods has to start with designing them in "ruthless pursuit of affordability," in the words of development entrepreneur Paul Polak.[186] If they can have some assurance that a market is likely to exist, developed-world private equity and venture capital can make a real difference upstream in the value chain by financing this design for affordability. By providing capital to the market for manufacturing of distributed energy components, including the manufacturing of standardized installation mechanisms, they can obtain significant returns on their investments, while lowering the price of components and innovating technologies to make them more saleable to the billions at the base of the pyramid.[187]

For truly innovative partnerships, such high-return–seeking investors can partner with some of the innovative firms that help companies create successful products for the developing world. Private consultancies such as IDEO and nonprofit–private partnerships such as those that exist around Stanford University's innovation labs can do the time-consuming research and design work, saving businesses money. For instance, Stanford's design school hosts a course, Entrepreneurial Design for Extreme Affordability, which spurred the solar power d.light Company that manufactures solar-powered lights to replace kerosene lamps.[188] After developing the d.light prototype in the Stanford class, the firm's founders secured $6 million in venture funding from a set of commercial firms looking to make real money on the $25 lamps.[189]

Venture firms can also help to segment the market so that it develops lower-capacity systems demanded by developing-country consumers at an attractive price.[190] Starting in 2005, feed-in tariffs and other solar-energy policies in developed countries such as Germany and Spain shifted the market toward developing larger capacity systems that met developed-country demand. The shift toward distributed generation in the developed world had a paradoxical effect in the short term: With reduced manufacturing capacity for the components needed for lower-capacity systems demanded by the developing world, the systems needed by the poor actually became more expensive for a period of time. Ultimately, of course, this explosion in the field was good for everyone—bringing down prices for photovoltaics by 40% in 2009–2010, and another 20% in 2011. Better market segmentation on the production side would have reduced the volatility in the developing world.

4) Build Demand through Quality Standards and Marketing Assistance

Affordability is not only about financial cost—it's also about opportunity cost, as well as about potential gain. It's possible to get small businesses and households to buy a costly but ultimately beneficial product. But as we've pointed out before, it becomes impossible if they see similar systems broken and unable to repay the initial investment, or unreliable and unable to meet their promised energy output. A history of cheap, poor-quality products has left some areas with a legacy of distrust for distributed generation.

Luckily, it is possible to market distributed generation with a quality standard. A respected local or international social-sector organization could create the equivalent of a "Good Housekeeping Seal of Approval" for high-quality products. A business consortium could do the same, provided its members were honest and worked together to self-police. Even a single individual business can stake its brand on quality control—and by doing so, differentiate itself and even charge a price premium, if the market will bear it. In Kenya, the Kenya Renewable Energy Association established a quality-assurance program that helped to reassure the market and that allowed its products to prosper.[191] Grameen Shakti alleviates market fears with a promise to buy back any system if the customer is not satisfied.

Marketing also requires demonstrating that individuals will gain from purchasing a new product. Grameen Shakti provides initial units free of charge to village leaders and other key influencers to generate some keeping-up-with-the-Joneses competition, as well as a demonstration effect.[192] In its own way, Grameen had hit on the same sexy viral marketing strategy used by fashion and accessories companies that fight to get celebrities to wear their shoes or carry their handbags! Social-sector organizations can also play a useful role in helping businesses learn marketing skills and segment the market and focus initially on businesses, wealthier consumers, and anchor tenants who can themselves sell off energy. Social-sector organizations can also build prototypes that show customers how the product can help them increase business income, and calculate potential consumer savings and how long a product will take to repay its initial cost. These market-facilitation measures are costly for small businesses, and hard for new entrepreneurs to even think about as they race to get their businesses off the ground. But they are essential, and relatively inexpensive, means of creating demand.

5) Train Installation and Maintenance Technicians

Before the distributed energy market takes off, it faces a chicken-and-egg problem with regard to a trained workforce. Businesses are more overhead-intensive if they must train their own workforce, inhibiting many from getting into the market. But few are going to buy a system if installation takes months and maintenance is patchy due to a bare-bones workforce.

There is a business opportunity in providing installation and ongoing maintenance, of course; that is one of the job-creating benefits of a market-led model. But just as few plumbing businesses train their own plumbers, and few contractors train their construction staff, it is hard to build a profitable business model that requires not just paying the salaries, but also conducting the initial training of a workforce. Eventually, private vocational schools can profit from training technicians to maintain and install distributed generation systems, as they do for other skilled trades throughout the developing world. But until a market exists, it is hard to generate enough students to make teaching profitable.

So in the early stages of the market, training a workforce is a role best played by either government-subsidized schools, or by social-sector organizations that can scale back their offerings as the private sector scales up. Once again, the Grameen family of organizations demonstrates the usefulness of this model. Grameen Shakti does not want to spend scarce capital on training. But other parts of the Grameen family of enterprises are nonprofit organizations with a different bottom line, as well as a deep reach into communities throughout Bangladesh. Drawing on these local networks, they recruited and trained a maintenance and sales force that eventually helped the for-profit company. As a social-sector organization, they focused on building an army of young women from user households and trained them in repair and maintenance, an effort with a triple payoff: They enabled these women to make a living, created a labor force that was trusted within their communities, and this labor force also played a further role in building demand. These "solar engineers" could be hired directly by the retailer or employed for an ongoing small maintenance contract with Grameen Shakti. Given the typical low wages of the young, this model not only ensured that products were well-maintained, it also kept the costs of installation and maintenance low to end consumers.[193] Grameen has also begun training women as solar technicians, so that they may also produce accessories for solar systems—an "apps" market that drives continual innovation, and will, like the solar engineers, be market-driven after Grameen provides the initial training.[194] Grameen understands that the creation of such a sales, maintenance, and innovation force is a crucial role it can play as a nonprofit venture that fuels a market-based solution.

Can getting these five elements right create a favorable environment for market-sector energy solutions anywhere on earth? We believe it can, in most circumstances, though the path to getting these elements right will differ in each country. However, given the decades long counterinsurgency that American forces have been waging perhaps the more pertinent question for U.S. policymakers is: Could such a market be created in Afghanistan to assist the country as US troops begin to leave? Certainly, nothing else has succeeded, after billions of dollars in investments from well-meaning donors trying to build centralized electricity-producing facilities. Despite burning summers and freezing winters, dark winter days and even darker winter nights, electricity has barely penetrated the country. Outside of the major cities, it rarely exists at all. Do these lessons of demand creation, business modeling, and other reforms have anything to teach us about how we could bring electricity to a desperately poor, war-torn country? For that, we turn to the next chapter.

"In Iraq, an issue that motivated fighters in some Baghdad neighborhoods was lack of adequate sewer, water, electricity, and trash services. Their concerns were totally disconnected from the overall Ba'athist goal of expelling U.S. forces and retaining Sunni Arab power."

— U.S. Army/Marine Corps Counterinsurgency Field Manual, pp. 15–16.

"In the last few years, supply lines have been increasingly threatened either by enemy action or through international crises, and in places like Kandahar [Afghanistan], where we have a large presence, we've been plugged into a very unsustainable and really an incapable grid system."

— Congresswoman Gabrielle Giffords, questioning General Petraeus, June 2010

Afghanistan:
Distributed Energy as Part of the Solution

It's hard to remember that as recently as the 1970s, Afghanistan was a stop on the hippie trail. Long-haired Westerners shopped for *tchotchkes* on Chicken Street and drove their VW buses through the heart of the country to visit the Buddhas of Bamiyan. Afghan engineers and professionals befriended their Western counterparts. Yet since the 1978 coup, the history of Afghanistan has been one of almost continuous and pervasive war. Today, while NATO and U.S. troops work to deny al Qaeda a safe haven in the country, Afghanistan remains a Hobbesian world where life is brutal, nasty, and (with a life expectancy of forty-four years) short.

If we had to pick an ideal place to introduce distributed energy, we would not start here! But to root out terrorism, the United States, at least initially, has chosen a policy of counterinsurgency. Multiple generals have made it clear that this war cannot be won solely on the battlefield, but will only be ended when the Afghan government has won the hearts and minds of a portion of the population, following counterinsurgency principles that make the protection of Afghan civilians paramount. In other words, to quell the insurgency, NATO forces are committed to a comprehensive strategy that helps Afghan civilians in order to bind their allegiance to NATO and to their own government.

A major element of this plan requires electricity. According to a recent paper by USAID's Afghan Clean Energy Program: "Only 10%–12% of the Afghan population has access to electricity; one of the lowest rates in the world. 340,000 customers are connected to the public power grid, of which 182,000 are in the Kabul area [out of approximately 3 million Kabul residents]. The other provinces have far less access to electricity, with rural areas being virtually un-served."[195] Meanwhile, 75% of all fuel in Afghanistan is firewood.[196] Harvesting wood for heat (and cooking fuel) is already fast depleting the oak forests that Afghans rely on for energy.[197] But running out of heat is not an option during winters that can reach −20°F—not if you want to survive.

Lack of electricity is a fundamental cause of Afghanistan's underdevelopment. Economic initiatives such as dried-fruit processing, almond growing, and all manner of pomegranate-based businesses are now being attempted to develop the country economically and as part of the counterinsurgency—but all require reliable energy to move beyond cottage industries.[198]

Lack of electricity also strongly correlates with lack of education and illiteracy.[199] This, in itself, has become a significant problem for coalition forces. Training the Afghan National

Army is essential for the U.S. and NATO to exit the country responsibly, with some assurance that local troops may keep insurgents from once again gaining a government apparatus from which to export terror. Yet well over 80% of the Afghan troops entering the national army are illiterate. The U.S. military has declared that literacy is "the essential enabler" for local forces' success.[200] As Lt. Gen. William Caldwell, head of the NATO-led effort to train the Afghan national security forces, explains: "How do you expect a soldier to account for their weapon if they can't even read the serial number?"[201] To enable NATO to turn the Afghanistan mission over to local forces, immediate literacy training is necessary. We can do this ourselves in the immediate term, in military bases lit with generators. Meanwhile, to ensure that the pipeline of local forces continues to be literate, we need children learning to read. That is possible without electricity—but given the short, cold winter days with less than six hours of sunlight (during which many children must tend to animals), and the difficulty of learning without air conditioning as summer temperatures creep over 120°F, much more probable with it.

Finally, electricity is needed for the allied war effort itself. Those generators needed to light and heat military bases come at a major cost. Insurgent attacks on the lumbering NATO fuel convoys are a significant cause of casualties to NATO forces; an Army study found that for every 24 fuel convoys that set out in Iraq or Afghanistan, one soldier or civilian was killed.[202] Stalled supply lines are routinely attacked, and given their fuel loads, are easily set ablaze.[203] Those supply lines are generally carrying fossil fuel, which accounts for between 30% and 80% of the convoy load in Afghanistan.[204] While some of that fuel is for vehicles, a significant portion runs diesel generators used by military forces for basic electricity and water purification, all of which could be replaced if local electricity existed. Meanwhile, the military might spend up to $400 for a gallon of gas in Afghanistan, once the fully burdened cost of fuel, including its transportation costs, are taken into account.[205] For this reason, the U.S. military has become a major funder of research and development into distributed generation technologies.

ELECTRICITY IN AFGHANISTAN: CENTRALIZED GENERATION FAILS, AND FAILS AGAIN

Afghanistan needs a lot of energy, fast. The Afghan government and international donors all recognize the problem. Under the government's draft plan for the Afghan electricity sector, access to electricity was supposed to grow to 25% by 2010, and to 33% by 2015, at which time 90% of the urban population was supposed to have access.[206] Despite the planning, at the 2010 milestone they were not even halfway toward their modest goal.

The government plan is based on centralized generation: rebuilding the existing grid and generation facilities, adding new transmission lines to import energy from nearby countries, and allowing some further growth of diesel generation in the short term, with a longer-term goal of replacing diesel with less costly and more environmentally friendly/sound alternatives.[207] The plan makes little sense—Afghanistan reportedly has very little energy internally. Its potential natural gas reserves are reported to be just over 120 billion cubic meters (less than the amount of energy it would take to power the U.S. for a single day), and it is estimated to have little more than 125 million tons of coal (just a little more than is burned by North Korea in a single year).[208] The North East Power System (NEPS) was supposed to provide 20%–25% of the power needs of the region based largely on importing power from Tajikistan, Uzbekistan, and Turkmenistan through newly built transmission lines. Yet Afghanistan has very little by way of foreign currency with which to purchase energy from foreign countries.

Nevertheless, outsiders, like the Afghan government, continue to turn to centralized generation as their solution. Over and over. For decades. In the 1950s, U.S. aid projects first entered Afghanistan to build the Kajaki Dam as part of an immense irrigation and canal project intended to help Afghanistan flower. Such projects began again almost as soon as allied troops entered Afghanistan following the first phase of the war in 2001. In 2002, a consortium of donors provided emergency financing for the energy sector. Later that year, a German donor provided funds for rehabilitating two hydropower plants, a substation in Kabul, and part of the distribution network. The World Bank began a program to restart another Kabul power plant, inactive for a decade and a half. And USAID began working with the Afghan government, international financial institutions, and the governments of Japan and India to repair and expand the centralized generation system while providing emergency fuel.[209]

Meanwhile, Americans returned to their 1950s-era Kajaki Dam project. They refurbished old turbines and got the plant running on partial power, but construction delays and safety failures prevented the installation of the new Chinese-built turbine.[210] Another large U.S. plan to build a major hydropower plant in the south has been delayed by fighting. In 2007, the U.S. rushed to build a power plant in Kabul—partially motivated by the hope that providing electricity to city residents plagued by constant blackouts would build optimism, gain the government legitimacy, and help President Karzai win reelection. The diesel-fueled power plant first saw construction lags that delayed work by more than a year, while costs rose from $100 million to more than $300 million. Capital expenditures aside, once the plant was completed the cost of the diesel fuel to power the plant was so expensive that it drove operating costs through the roof. The cost of delivering diesel across war-torn supply lines led to operating costs at the plant that were seven times higher than the six cents per kilowatt-hour that it costs to bring in power from neighboring countries along transmission lines.[211] In other words, the U.S. spent hundreds of millions of dollars to produce power at a price too costly to use and, as a result, the plant has largely sat idle since construction was finished. The Afghan Deputy Minister of Water and Energy remarked at the time: "Instead of giving me a small car, you give me really a Jaguar. . . . And it will be up to me whether I use it, or just park it and look at it."[212]

Newspaper reports about the U.S. project described it as foundering on shoddy construction, corruption, and cost overruns—but those are icing on the cake of more fundamental problems with centralized generation as a strategy. First, as the Deputy Minister pointed out after the fact, Afghanistan lacks money to sustain such projects: As a country that ranks in the bottom 5% in GDP per capita, Afghanistan has been running on foreign aid since 2001. As such, developing an electricity infrastructure that requires large sums of money to sustain and expand is foolhardy: It creates a situation in which Afghanistan will be saddled with a system that it cannot perpetuate once the international assistance dries up. The costs of creating and sustaining centralized power are simply too much for such a country to bear.

Yet even if international donors were willing to fund and subsidize Afghanistan's electrical system for decades to come, centralized generation is not a workable solution. There are reasons why centralized generation has never gained much ground in Afghanistan. The core problems are threefold: terrain, population distribution, and governance.

Dominated by range after range of imposing mountains, Afghanistan has only one paved road that connects most major cities—the Ring Road built by Coalition forces after the fall of the Taliban. Attempting to build a spider's web of transmission lines across such harsh land in the midst of a war might not be impossible, but it would be close. Oil and gas pipelines would entail engineering more difficult than the groundbreaking Alaska pipeline in order to navigate both the mountains and the broad temperature swings that cause expansion, contraction, and breakage. Moving fuel overland would require rail lines or roads that do not exist and would require vast expenditures to make them resilient to the harsh climate—as well as secure against bombs and attacks. Centralized generation can work in Kabul, and a few other major cities—but without vast sums of money, and long stretches of peace, it cannot spread throughout the country.

Unlike many developing countries whose citizenry is largely clustered in densely packed urban areas, Afghanistan is not highly urbanized or centralized. Only about 24% of the population lives in urban centers.[213] More than three-quarters of the population reside in small villages clustered throughout the remote countryside.[214] Population density is low: about 42 people per square kilometer.[215] As such, even if the government was successful in providing Kabul or Kandahar with reliable electricity, the vast majority of Afghans would still be without. Pouring resource after resource and international dollar after international dollar into electrifying Kabul will do nothing to develop the 75% of the population that lives elsewhere and, correspondingly, will do nothing to win the fight for hearts and minds in the places this fight matters most: the villages.

Finally, there is governance—a euphemism for the reality that Afghanistan has been at war for over three decades, in anarchic government conditions—and that as of 2010, it ranked third to last in Transparency International's corruption index, beating out only Somalia and Myanmar. No matter how successful the current NATO effort is, it is almost certain that there will be a portion of the population who wish to undermine the government and destabilize population areas. Even if a centralized facility could be protected, every mile of transmission line, oil or gas pipeline, or transport road represents a point of vulnerability and a potential target for an insurgent fighter. According to a study led by Dr. Hisham Zerriffi at the University of British Columbia, when stress, particularly conflict-induced stress, is accounted for in economic models, distributed generation is significantly more reliable than centralized generation.[216] Such findings ring true in Afghanistan: In Helmand Province, power from the centralized Kajaki power plant has been disrupted six times between January and July of 2010, each time forcing talks with the local Taliban.[217]

Moreover, it is not simply that insurgents target power plants for destruction: In Afghanistan they are also using the little centralized power that exists for economic gain. The U.S. poured $100 million into doubling the capacity of the Kajaki hydropower plant, the main source of electricity for southern Afghanistan. As described above, only a few of the old, refurbished turbines could be made to work. And even then, in Helmand Province where half of that electricity flows, the Taliban have enough control of the population centers to force Afghans to pay their utility bills directly to the insurgency. The Taliban go door to door collecting payments, cutting off electricity of those who refuse to match the amounts they pay to the government. Meanwhile, they have also stolen electricity from the main lines to extend power to villages they control, in their own effort to win hearts and minds.[218]

THE PROMISE AND PITFALLS OF DISTRIBUTED GENERATION

One would think that such inherent problems with centralized generation would have led the government and donors to consider other methods. Yet while the Afghan government's 2007 energy plan recognized that some renewable energy might be useful, projects have been small-scale. The Asian Development Bank (ADB) offered $750,000 to investigate solar energy.[219] A tiny program is under way to train ten "barefoot solar engineers" who will then train ten others, and so on, to install and maintain solar systems. Other nonprofit aid organizations have invested in pilot hydroelectric and wind projects. The few million dollars that international donors have spent on such distributed energy projects is a pittance compared with the hundreds of millions poured into failed centralized generation facilities. Distributed generation is conceived of as feel-good aid and charity directed at households, rather than as a serious means to generate large-scale electricity for the country to fuel economic rebirth.

One of the only entities that seems serious about distributed generation is the National Solidarity Program (NSP)—tellingly, a program whose aid projects are conceived and run by local villages. Financed by the Afghan government with World Bank funds, the NSP provides block grants to villages. To receive the grants, villagers "must elect a village Community Development Council, and a quorum of the village must meet to reach a consensus on priority projects, and accounts must be posted in a public place" to avoid corruption.[220] NSP projects have been undertaken by tens of thousands of villages, and in many parts of Afghanistan NSP is the only functioning government development program.[221] Many of these villages have chosen to implement power projects, often micro-hydro dams, believing that small-scale electricity is something that they desire more than any other good they could communally provide. In fact, villages implemented so many micro-energy programs that there has been a "mini-boom for [micro-hydro power] MHP-related services in the country."[222] According to a 2009 on-the-ground study conducted by Linton Wells II, the Director of the Center for Technology and National Security Policy at National Defense University: "Between the start of the NSP and 2006 more than 300 MHP projects were either started or completed throughout 22 provinces."[223] The German development agency GTZ has also been supportive of distributed generation, particularly micro-hydro, not as pure aid, but as a viable source of economically productive energy. GTZ recognizes that even limited electrical supplies stimulate an economic renaissance in isolated communities.[224]

As GTZ and these Afghans know, distributed renewable generation has a great deal of potential. First, it can be generated relatively quickly—showing results in months, or even weeks. That is important in a country where the U.S. needs electricity immediately for war fighting, and wants to show an impact during the few years that we remain in the country. The effect of this immediacy can be profound. In a country used to broken promises, where the government has promised much but delivered little, it provides a tangible representation of the benefits of supporting the elected government or NATO forces. Moreover, even small-scale electricity can quickly impact life—not just allowing children to study and adults to work in the evening, but also creating opportunities for cottage industry and other economic development. Finally, small-scale projects can evade some of the pervasive corruption of Afghanistan. Large projects with enormous budgets provide greater opportunities for malfeasance—and more chance that such corruption will not be discovered—than smaller, more localized projects.

These potentially positive aspects of distributed generation must be qualified. Quickly delivered, shoddily implemented products by aid contractors that simply provide a product rather than building local capacity can do more harm than good. And, unfortunately, the U.S. has a strong record of projects along these lines. For instance, a million-dollar canal built with U.S. assistance was intended to bring water to a new hydroelectric facility in Badakhshan. But the realities of contractor projects in the Afghan war zone—cost overruns, high staff turnover, security risks, and demand for speed—left a shoddy trench that did not work to provide electricity—and further soured Afghans on waste, corruption, secrecy, and the U.S. ability to implement what it promised.[225]

The Badakhshan failure is not an anomaly. It is estimated that fewer than 10% of the micro-hydro plants built in Afghanistan—many as part of the National Solidarity Program—are still working.[226] Most became silted up and were left unmaintained until they were unusable. Other mid-sized projects have met similar fates.

If energy is so needed in Afghanistan, why are perfectly good dams being wasted? A bit of investigation places us squarely back in the litany of problems cited in Chapter Three.

First, micro-hydro is quite complex. Each system requires specific siting and technical expertise. A survey completed in 2006 found that demand for micro-hydro often exceeded local manufacturing and engineering supply, leading to many projects that failed to meet minimal standards for performance and sustainability. Much of the technology was of poor quality, while the planning schemes too often exceeded the technical capacities of local talent.[227]

Systems as technically complex as micro-hydro also require hard choices between cost and sustainability. Many pieces require local construction—and cheap construction means systems work less well, silt more quickly, and break more frequently. While most parts of the system can be produced locally, and some parts, such as turbines, are beginning to be standardized, generators cannot be obtained locally at all. The generator, however, is the part of a micro-hydro project that most frequently needs replacing. So projects must decide between buying higher-quality components from Japan, or products from China or Pakistan that are one-fifth the cost. While an outside donor could subsidize the first purchase of a fancier part, locals will have far more trouble raising the funds for subsequent purchases of more expensive replacement generators—the kind of capital-cost problem that can cause a $30,000 micro-hydro project to be left to fail for want of a $2,000 replacement generator.[228]

Finally, social issues loom large for village-level projects that require significant ongoing maintenance. Because of the cost, size, and site requirements of projects, most micro-hydro must be implemented on a village rather than on an individual or family level. But village-level programs can fail to provide the sense of ownership that ensures the maintenance of personal or family-owned items. Meanwhile, NSP programs often did not factor in funds for maintenance—not only to pay for new systems, but to pay someone to maintain them. While it is idealistic to believe that a village would pitch in to maintain a project for the common good, in a low-trust society such as Afghanistan, where social structures have been decimated by conflict, refugee life, and the breakdown of traditional power structures, such a hope cannot be relied on. Moreover, in many micro-hydro programs, there is not enough power for everyone. The local *shura* must often decide who gets what—which can lead to ethnic, class, and other divisions.

So, is distributed generation an idea that is dead on arrival for Afghanistan? Should we throw up our hands at this country ever having electricity, if centralized and decentralized options have failed? Or are there lessons that can be applied from the previous chapters to let light into Afghanistan?

It's true that Afghanistan is a particularly difficult developing country for introducing and selling a new product—and not only because of poverty and war. Having three-quarters of the population distributed throughout tiny villages makes it hard for new technology to catch on and spread. Low trust levels also impede the uptake of new ideas. Travel is slow at best, dangerous at worst, making it hard to sell or maintain products in even nearby villages.[229] Moreover, given the low population densities outside the larger cities, local businesses cannot make a profit selling just to those located nearby. Finally, corruption is so pervasive that it acts as a significant tax on business, reducing the tiny margins that exist.

Hard, however, does not mean impossible. It may be difficult to get distributed energy to the farthest flung of Afghanistan's villages, but that does not mean it is not worth starting such projects and at least spreading them to the urban and peri-urban areas, which are also in need of electricity. The Taliban threat, after all, is amid some of the easier-to-reach parts of the country, and spreads its tendrils right to the suburbs of Kabul. And the magic of distributed generation, as opposed to centralized generation, is that from these urban and peri-urban areas, the technology can slowly spread to more rural regions linked by a friend, a cousin, or a business partner. Even in a low-trust culture, ideas can catch on. A friend running a humanitarian organization in Afghanistan recalls trying to introduce a laser-leveling device to farmers that would allow them to grade their fields absolutely flat. They were uninterested in the technology, until he brought them together to a demonstration field that had been leveled with the laser, and gave it a small amount of water. The water spread evenly and covered the whole field, with no painstaking work and no loss of the precious liquid. Suddenly, demand was generated. The risk-averse farmers saw what a laser-level could do for them—and how a collective purchase could be of benefit to them all. The next step is when the farmers who buy the level start outproducing the ones who don't, and that is even more exciting. Like the shopkeeper who can stay open longer or the restaurateur who serves cold beer, increased output and sales lead to higher rates of product adoption. Be it laser-levels or solar panels, this is how a market is born— even in Afghanistan.

A SUCCESSFUL PROGRAM FOR BRINGING DISTRIBUTED ENERGY TO AFGHANISTAN

So what would a successful program for introducing distributed energy to Afghanistan look like? First, it should start in the cities and their surrounding areas, where ideas can spread more easily, and businesses can attain a large enough customer base to gain profitability. It should also focus on business-to-business sales, for all the reasons mentioned in the preceding chapter. Once businesses are profitable, they can find ways to move a sales, installation, and maintenance force to rural areas—but it makes sense to start with low-hanging fruit.

Next, different sectors should be activated to play the various roles that they play best. Development banks and bilateral aid institutions should focus on creating a playing field on which business can play. They should work on the regulatory framework to reduce any potential import duties on distributed generation products, and to allow the market to operate in the distributed energy sector. Afghanistan's 1980 Enterprises Act was drawn up under the Soviet puppet government and created five enterprises to manage the electricity sector, each of them heavy with bureaucracy and light on expertise.[230] Development banks can work with the government to cut this red tape and open room for a market.

They should then focus on bringing in capital that can invest in local business at a scalable level. Micro-credit may help the poorest of the poor—but in this case, aid and development banks should be aiming to provide capital for larger businesses that can scale to provide energy services—products, installation, and/or maintenance—to large neighborhoods or cities. In the best-case scenario, development banks would provide risk insurance and a co-investor to attract private capital, possibly from nearby China and India, which would have much to gain by expanding its markets for PV, wind, and other distributed products they manufacture. While we wish we could suggest buying American, it will destroy uptake of the technology for Afghans to have to wait for shipments of parts from America each time they need a repair. China, whose solar products are 25%–50% cheaper than those in Europe, and which also benefits from its closer location for heavier products such as wind turbines, simply makes more business sense.[231]

Meanwhile, nonprofit social-sector organizations can create the conditions in which local businesses can thrive. As organizations that can gain trust and work on the ground with a good feel for local human capital, nonprofits can excel at providing one-on-one training, and partnering with vocational schools and universities to create programs in the installation and maintenance of various types of distributed energy systems most suited to different regions of Afghanistan. In some cases, such as with wood gasification systems, social-sector organizations can teach how to build and maintain systems.

In systems that cannot be manufactured locally, such as PV, they can work with the entire supply chain to try to reduce costs and ensure high-quality products.[232] Pioneering social-sector organizations such as Ashoka have already begun such work, which they term "hybrid value chains" to describe the partnership between private and nonprofit actors to create market value and social value simultaneously through the creation of products that can be sold to the poor for their benefit.[233] In fact, it was in partnership with Ashoka that Cemex, the Mexican cement company we described earlier, developed its sales force for its room-by-room cement products. As mentioned in the last chapter, social-sector organizations can assist businesses by investing in marketing and demonstration models. By training businesses in sales; helping to create a trained, high-quality group of installers and maintenance workers; and building a value chain that gets products to market in the cheapest possible manner while maintaining high quality, social-sector organizations can play a pivotal role in allowing a market to materialize.

Finally, local entrepreneurs should be engaged to take advantage of the capital provided by external investors, and start businesses that provide distributed energy products, as Zara Solar has done in Tanzania. These businesses should start with a business-to-business model, focusing their first sales efforts on large and small businesses that need power, not on homeowners. By selling first to businesses, distributed energy technology will benefit from a demonstration effect, which can help generate greater economic activity across the nation. The household market, which is more far-flung, more price-sensitive, and requires less power per transaction, should come only after the business market, given the greater cost of maintaining and installing each unit. The low penetration of electrical appliances in most households means that electricity will largely be used in the evening for lighting, cell-phone charging, and some entertainment, making cost recovery difficult for energy providers. In many cases, secondary businesses that purchase distributed generation power and sell it again to householders—like the Grameen Bank village phones in Bangladesh—may start naturally. Again, social-sector organizations can play a role by helping pair local entrepreneurs with established entrepreneurs in nearby countries, such as Pakistan, Iran, and India, who can provide mentorship and advice from within business situations that bear more in common with Afghan than with Western markets. They can also assist with the collection of monthly installment fees, possibly through the National Solidarity Program.

Is this pie in the sky? Hardly. In Kabul, perhaps 1,000 small businesses already exist in which diesel-generator operators provide electricity to local neighbors, charging by the light-bulb to provide access to power. In the summer of 2010, powering a lightbulb cost about $2.60 a month, while keeping a television on cost nearly $11—in a country where the average income hovers around a dollar a day.[234] But these businesses found customers. Transforming them from diesel-generator businesses to renewable energy businesses is not an inconceivable proposition. Nor are these costs confined to urban areas: The Asian Development Bank estimates that rural Afghans spend approximately 25% of their household income on energy.[235] In the words of the Ministry of Energy and Water in 2007: "Afghan consumers are aware of the real electricity costs and are willing (and in many cases) able to pay for a reliable supply of acceptable quality."[236]

But what about theft, corruption, and the war itself? These are, of course, deterrents to business. They make it harder. But they don't make it impossible. Take the flood of cell phones into the country. As recently as 2001, there was not a single cell phone in Afghanistan. Afghans who lacked a landline and wished to make phone calls had to gather at a handful of government-run Public Calling Offices. But in 2003, the relative peace lured major global telecom companies to enter the market.[237] Now, four large private companies compete with a state-run enterprise for cell-phone business.[238] More than one-third of the Afghan population has a cell-phone account—and the market generates more than a billion dollars in annual revenue, according to government estimates. Does the war affect these companies? Yes, it causes all sorts of disruption. The Taliban bomb towers and force night-time shutoffs in various localities. But it has not come close to killing a profitable industry that has added immense benefit to the lives of millions of Afghan customers and the more than 100,000 people employed by the industry.[239] Meanwhile, Afghans direct real anger toward the Taliban for destroying something that is adding benefit to their lives—exactly the kind of reaction a counterinsurgency strategy is trying to gain through aid projects that both help the population and create animosity toward insurgents.

The immense penetration of cell phones creates a ready market for distributed generation. After all, these phones need to be charged, providing an immediate incentive for small-scale power for a large swath of the population.[240] Distributed generation cannot only profit from their business model, but from their business.

A "TO-DON'T" LIST

It is as important to note what we are *not* suggesting, as what we are. We do not believe that nonprofit organizations should provide and install distributed technology to help these poor villages. Nor should the U.S. government, aid donors, the U.S. military, or the Afghan government subsidize these technologies at first.[241] Of course, the government may eventually be needed to provide small capital subsidies to small subsets of the population such as the most rural poor (it is worth remembering that even America subsidized the installation of rural electricity through the Tennessee Valley Authority in the 1930s and 1940s). But beginning with government subsidies to pay for the ongoing cost of renewable energy will distort the market, require funds the Afghan government does not have, and inevitably garner charges of ethnic or regional favoritism that can be toxic in the current environment.

Finally, what we are suggesting is a market-based strategy. While villages could purchase technology as a group, our strategic suggestions for Afghanistan do not explicitly provide for village-level projects such as those supported by the NSP. We are not overtly opposed to these projects as we are to government subsidies or technology dumps, because of the

positive effects that tying villages together toward a common
goal can have. Clare Lockhart of the Institute for State
Effectiveness has written on the social capital and growing writ of the government that blossomed in Afghanistan
from distributed energy projects undertaken through the
National Solidarity Program.[242] These are significant side
effects with real meaning in the developing world, where, as
Robert Putnam noted, a trust deficit may be a crucial cause
of underdevelopment.[243] However, the problems with micro-
hydro demonstrate some of the obstacles to success in larger,
village-level projects in Afghanistan, particularly. Issues of
class, power, and distribution, as well as questions of who is in
charge of maintenance, can poison village-owned programs
in a low-trust society such as Afghanistan. Village-owned
projects may be more likely to face theft, because they are
not protected by individual families. Even projects that have
few parts available for theft, such as micro-hydro, can falter
because of a failure to have the buy-in that family ownership creates. In Afghanistan, wherever possible, the owners,
protectors, and users of energy should be the same people, to
ensure the greatest resilience.[244] That is what a market-based
solution provides.

Despite these simple lessons, America is on the verge of
getting into this market in the wrong way. Right now,
it is the military who may bring distributed generation to
Afghanistan—and that presents a number of problems.

U.S. Marines in Helmand Province are now testing a portable solar system to run lights, provide shade, and charge
computers and communications equipment.[245] Their goal

is to help smaller sites and forward operating bases be self-sustaining with power that can be generated on the battle-field, not shipped from Karachi through narrow mountain passes.[246] For the military to develop distributed energy technology for its own uses is a terrific idea, and could yield real savings in lives as well as in dollars. But there is talk of providing enough energy that the military could help nearby villages located near forward operating bases, by providing them with excess power. Other officers dream of using Commander's Emergency Response Program (CERP) funds to help villages buy distributed energy as part of their counterinsurgency strategy.[247] Their motives to help villages, and to show that good things can come from American and NATO troops, are impeccable. But what they would do, in actuality, is harm the chances of a market taking hold. By providing technology with no funds and no one trained to take on ongoing maintenance, they would ensure that dere-lict projects would be left unused across Afghanistan as soon as a part breaks. The presence of these forgotten systems, such as the defunct micro-hydro projects, in turn, could dis-courage the uptake of distributed energy for decades to come. The best of intentions could yield the worst of results.

The potential impact that renewable generation could have on the developing world, including post-conflict environ-ments, is immeasurable. It has the possibility to quickly and effectively harness local, renewable energy sources to bring electricity to those with little hope of ever being con-nected to a centralized grid. It has the ability to bring com-munities together and bind the allegiances of its citizens to the elected government. In Afghanistan this translates not just into more tacit supporters of the government, but rather supporters who are willing to actively fight against the Taliban in order to protect their newfound way of life. There are no silver bullets in a counterinsurgency just as there are no silver bullets in the fight to bring people out of poverty. There are, however, tactics and strategies that work better than others. Renewable distributed energy has the real possibility to be one of those that simply works better—in both counterinsurgencies as well as in standard developing nations. If done right, it has the potential to bring light to those who have known only darkness during the night and perhaps to even play a role in bringing peace to people who have known only war.

"Fortunes have been made on the back of that cellphone business. A decade ago you wouldn't have imagined you could target these populations, but there is real business opportunity in introducing the right technologies."

—Bill Reichert, venture capitalist[248]

Conclusion

Electricity is a miracle most of us take for granted. We walk through our front door after a long day at work, flip a switch—and in an instant what was once shrouded in darkness is awash in light. On any given evening, we might use electricity to watch television, cook dinner, charge our cell phones, or all three at once, while typing emails on our computer and engaging in the myriad other small tasks that require instant access to electricity. Most of us never give this miracle a second thought.

We all know there are "other" people living in "other" places who don't have it so good. Their homes have no lights or light switches. Animal dung and wood fires fuel their cookstoves. And their work, if they can get it, is manual labor performed with no help from the thousands of electronic assists that increase our productivity and earning power. The plight of these people might cross our minds from a humanitarian perspective, as a charity might tug at our heartstrings. But should we be concerned for other reasons?

The failure to provide energy to the developing world, a hundred years after its spread to a good chunk of humanity, is a tragedy. The world loses the ingenuity and ability of more than 1.5 million people a year who die from the effects of indoor air pollution. The economic life of developing countries is stunted, while desertification, air pollution, and climate change take their inexorable toll on the landscape. But the problem of providing energy is not simply a matter of international charity. The threat multiplication effects of climate refugees are exacerbating international tensions, from the Bangladesh/India border to the volatile region that splits the Muslim north of Africa from its Christian and animist south. The developing world's reliance on oil for electricity as well as transportation fuel adds to the oil demand that entrenches regimes inimical to the United States. Finally, our ability to win hearts and minds as a counterinsurgency tactic depends in part on our ability to make peoples' lives palpably better: a win that electricity can provide in regions where it did not previously exist such as Afghanistan, and where our failure to provide what existed before is a clear mark of failure in the eyes of the population we are trying to win over in places such as Iraq.

For decades, development professionals and developing-world governments have tried to meet these needs through centralized generation. In some cases, such as in parts of Latin America and Asia, they have succeeded. But in many, many places, for many, many years, they have failed. In case after case, governments have made grand plans to electrify their countries. Aided by international banks, they have indebted their countries for planned plants that too often failed to materialize. At best, such plants were built—generally over budget and years late—only to be beset by lack of maintenance, theft, subsidies, harsh climatic conditions, conflict, and a dozen other pitfalls that render them less and less able to meet the power needs of their population.

Distributed generation takes a different tack. Rather than requiring central government decisions and years of politically fraught planning, these energy sources can be up and running almost immediately, after a market is established. And like laptop computers, a small-scale solution taken up by the masses can actually have a greater reach than grand plans that never become reality. Yet distributed generation has also been slow to catch on since the technologies were first pioneered a few decades ago. While the inability of distributed generation to emerge as a strong element of electrification strategy has not left countries deeply indebted financially as the failures of centralized power have, it has also not managed to catapult to scale.

We believe that this failure can be reversed if governments, donors, and international banks stop seeing it as their role to drop subsidized technology on the developing world, and instead start building markets. Instead of seeing themselves as one-stop shops that will provide the A-to-Z solution, from technology provision to installation, maintenance, and training, (international) development donors and nonprofits can leverage their unique capabilities to create market friendly environments in which local businesses can thrive. Not only is this the only way to scale solutions, it also catalyzes economic growth through the jobs created by the energy market itself.

The case studies we have highlighted on successful (and unsuccessful) business models in the developing world shed light on what works and what pitfalls to avoid. Markets are easiest to begin with business-to-business sales, so that end users can both get the micro-financing that will enable them to purchase equipment and so that their businesses can provide demonstration effects that encourage others to enter the market. They can and should move on to selling to consumers—and in that case, because economies of scale are crucial for low-margin products sold to the poor—markets must begin where there are concentrations of people. It is hard to turn over enough product to support a viable business when selling in sparsely populated rural areas.[249] These areas may be reached later, as the market matures—or they may eventually require subsidies for locales where there simply is not a viable market-based way to sell goods. But they should not be where businesses begin. On that note, businesses must segment the market, likely starting with higher-end consumers who can afford the upfront costs. Finally, building demand is crucial. Even free energy does not sell itself. The local businesses most likely to succeed are those with dense local networks they can draw upon to both generate demand and enable strong distribution channels.

Meanwhile, what local businesses can do, social-sector organizations should not do. Most crucially, neither nonprofits nor aid donors and governments should be in the business of directly providing and installing distributed energy systems—especially subsidizing systems themselves—to anyone but the absolute poorest of the poor. Providing such subsidized technology inhibits the market, taking crucial market share away from budding entrepreneurs. In other words, unless nonprofits wish to provide electricity to the majority of the 1.5 billion unelectrified poor, they should stop providing aid that prevents the market from doing just that. Meanwhile, providing such systems to the poorest of the poor before those who can afford to buy are enabled to do so by the market will create jealousy, difficult social relationships in villages, and can even stigmatize new technology—suggesting that even these marginal subsidies, where they are absolutely necessary, should be used only after a market is already in place. Nonprofits, aid donors, and governments should also not engage in showcase projects in areas with no trained workforce. Such efforts tend to leave behind highly visible, broken systems that remain white elephants, casting their chilling shadow over the market for decades. Conducting demonstration projects is a fine thing for a nonprofit to do, but these projects should be focused on creating demand for electricity, not on creating the electricity itself.

Where subsidies are useful, they are not focused on consumers, or on providing technology—but are directed at the other end of the supply chain to encourage the production of cheap, high-quality local products, where a manufacturing base has the possibility of success. Such subsidies to manufacturing businesses combined with quality-control programs have been successful in China in bringing down cost while using their leverage to increase quality, helping to ensure that poor-quality products don't destroy the infant stages of a market.[250]

That does not mean that social-sector organizations', aid, and government efforts have no role to play in distributed generation. In fact, without them, a market friendly environment cannot exist. The U.S. Government, other governments, and social-sector organizations can and must play a myriad of supporting roles to jumpstart a market in distributed energy—they must simply be the supporting roles that create an enabling business environment. From working with governments to privatize, deregulate, reduce tariffs, and otherwise open up a market, to training a workforce, helping businesses with marketing and technology development, and assisting with soft financing and micro-credit; social-sector enterprises, international banks, and development organizations are essential to creating the environment that allows a market to thrive.

The payoff from such a strategy could well be the provision of electricity to millions, possibly more than a billion, people who live without light in the darkness. While the world continues to debate climate change, and the West remains addicted to oil and coal, the developing world could pioneer the widespread adoption of a leapfrog technology that can help it to save itself. A single, 50-watt solar home system can replace about a one-quarter ton of carbon dioxide per year, according to conservative estimates. Multiply those effects across just half of those living without power, and nearly 200 million tons of carbon dioxide would be saved each year. The vision of developing-world countries taking their fate into their own hands echoes Gandhi's cries for self-sufficiency. Distributed generation allows a country to pick itself up by its bootstraps and create conditions in which its students can study longer, its people are healthier, and its enterprises can scale and grow. In contrast to centralized power, it lets poor countries with willing leadership shake themselves free from subsidies, aid, and debt, and create working economies. And it's a market that could enrich those who invest in some of the poorest parts of the world. It's an idea whose time has come.

Notes

1. General David Petraeus, Harvard Kennedy School, Cambridge, April 21, 2009, speech.

2. Brett Blackledge, Richard Lardner, and Deb Riechmann, "After years of Rebuilding, Most Afghans Lack Power," *The Associated Press*, July 19, 2010. http://www.msnbc.msn.com/id/38303355/ns/world_news-south_and_central_asia/38379217

3. General Gordon R. Sullivan, Admiral Frank Bowman, Lieutenant General Lawrence P. Farrell, Jr., Vice Admiral Paul G. Gaffney II, General Paul J. Kern, Admiral T. Joseph Lopez, Admiral Donald L. Pilling, Admiral Joseph W. Prueher, Vice Admiral Richard H. Truly, General Charles F. Wald, and General Anthony C. Zinni, "National Security and the Threat of Climate Change," The CNA Corporation, 2007.

4. David Victor and Richard K. Morse, "Living with Coal: Climate Policy's Most Inconvenient Truth," *Boston Review*, September/October 2009. http://bostonreview.net/BR34.5/victor_morse.php

5. Louisa Lim, "China's Coal-Fueled Boom has Costs," *National Public Radio*, May 2007. http://www.npr.org/templates/story/story.php?storyId=9947668

6. See "The Tormented Isthmus," *The Economist*, April 16, 2011.

7. "Aid to Pakistan by the Numbers," Center for Global Development. http://www.cgdev.org/section/initiatives/_active/pakistan/numbers After this funding was allocated, Pakistani floods and other political effects altered the prioritization of this aid funding toward urgent humanitarian needs rather than more long-term development goals.

8. Glenn Zorpette, "Struggling for Power in Afghanistan," *The New York Times*, July 5, 2011. http://www.nytimes.com/2011/07/06/opinion/06zorpette.html?_r=2&pagewanted=1

9. Distributed generation is a term with many definitions, and is described in greater detail in Chapter 2. We use it to refer to energy creation that is not centrally dispatched. Renewable distributed generation, our particular focus, includes all technologies that only minimally exacerbate global warming, from micro-hydropower to wind, solar, geothermal, and some biomass. Distributed generation generally refers to energy solutions that work for households or individual businesses and produce less than 20 megawatts per operation, but it can refer to the production of up to 300 megawatts—enough to power a small village.

10. Yaroslav Trofimov, "Cell Carriers Bow to Taliban Threat," *The Wall Street Journal*, March 23, 2010. http://online.wsj.com/article/SB1000142405274870411730457513754146523 5972.html

11. "The State of the World Population 2001, Meeting the Needs of the Poor and Protecting the Environment," United Nations Population Fund. http://www.unfpa.org/swp/2001/presskit/english/povertyen.htm

12. Alexandra Niez, "Comparative Study on Rural Electrification Policies in Emerging Economies," International Energy Agency, March 2010, p. 12.

13. Ibid., 12.

14. Ibid., 12.

15. External groups have spent approximately $4.6 billion on malaria eradication between 2003 and 2009, and annual commitments for

2008–2010 have stabilized at about $1.6 billion per year. "Malaria Funding & Resource Utilization: The First Decade of Roll Back Malaria," Roll Back Malaria, World Health Organization, 2010, pp. 11–12. http://www.rollbackmalaria.org/ProgressImpactSeries/docs/RBMMalariaFinancingReport-en.pdf

16. Rachel Bernstein, "Genetic modification makes mosquitoes malaria-proof," The *Seattle Times*, July 16, 2010. http://seattletimes.nwsource.com/html/nationworld/2012378603_malaria17.html

17. "10 Facts on Malaria," World Health Organization. http://www.who.int/features/factfiles/malaria/en/index.html

18. "Implications of Energy Poverty on Health & Environment: Harmful Effects of Current Cooking Fuels and Technologies," International Energy Agency. http://www.iea.org/weo/implication.asp

19. Ibid.

20. "World Energy Outlook 2006," International Energy Agency, p. 427.

21. Ibid., 427. Distributed generation cannot tackle all parts of this problem. While electricity has the ability to provide for heat, cooking, and light, most distributed generation programs are used for light and plugging in other electric goods, such as cell phones. Some may be used to displace other sources of heat energy. Rarely is distributed generation to provide electricity used to replace cooking over fire; cultural issues related to cooking styles play too large a role. However, distributed energy technologies, such as solar power cook stoves, can follow the same method as that we suggest—and are having an impact on particulate matter from cooking. See the Global Alliance for Clean Cookstoves for further information on these efforts.

22. Veerabhadran Ramanathan and Paul Crutzen, "The Asian Brown Cloud: Climate and Other Environmental Impacts," United Nations Environment Program Study, August 2002.

23. "Selected Issues in the Forest Sector: State of the World's Forests," Food and Agricultural Organization of the United Nations, 2007, p. 98.

24. "Facts and Figures," United Nations Environment Program. http://www.unep.fr/energy/activities/reed/pdf/energy-facts.pdf

25. Rhett A. Butler, "Nigeria has worst deforestation rate, FAO revises figures," *Mongabay.com*, November 17, 2005. http://news.mongabay.com/2005/1117-forests.html

26. Forest Sourcebook: Practical Guidance for Sustaining Forests in Development Cooperation Washington, D.C.: The World Bank 2008, p. 96.

27. "Energy and Agriculture," Sustainable Bioenergy Development in UEMOA Member Countries, October 2008, p. 34. Geneva: International Centre for Trade and Sustainable Development.

28. "Patterns of Rape in Darfur," Center on Law and Globalization. http://clg.portalxm.com/library/keytext.cfm?keytext_id=141

29. Anthony Nyong, "Climate Related Conflicts in West Africa," Environmental Change and Securities Program: The Wilson International Center for Scholars, Issue 12, 2006–2007, pp. 36–43.

30. Ibid.

31. Edmund Sanders, "Feeling Drought in the Horn of Africa," *Los Angeles Times*, October 25, 2009. http://articles.latimes.com/2009/oct/25/world/fg-climate-refugees25

32. Tara Bahrampour, "Out of Suburbia, the Online Extremist," The *Washington Post*, November 2, 2010. http://www.washingtonpost.com/wp-dyn/content/article/2010/11/01/AR2010110107035.html. See also Dina Temple Raston, "Indictments Widen US–Somali Terror Case," *National Public Radio*, August 5, 2010. http://www.npr.org/templates/story/story.php?storyId=129000435

33. The Horn of Africa joint task force grew out of Operation Enduring Freedom–Horn of Africa, as part of the U.S. response to the September 11, 2001, terrorist attacks. The Horn of Africa's proximity to the wahaabist fundamentalist interpretation of Islam in Gulf states, combined with negligible governance, has made countries such as Somalia front-line states for terrorist

development. The Joint Task Force Horn of Africa focuses on what U.S. leaders call an "indirect approach"—which combines development assistance, military training, and support for governments—to help stabilize the region.

34. The global, commoditized nature of the oil market means that regardless of where oil is purchased, when the price rises, it enriches these countries. In 2008, 60% of Iran's GDP came from global oil sales, while Russia's oil and gas accounted for between 10% and 30% of its GDP and 60% of its exports. Paul Abelsky, "Russian GDP Grew 2.9% Last Quarter on Stimulus, Oil (Update2)," Bloomberg Businessweek, May 14, 2010. http://www.businessweek.com/news/2010-05-14/russian-gdp-grew-2-9-last-quarter-on-stimulus-oil-update2-.html. See also, "Long-term Fiscal Sustainability of the Russian Federation," The World Bank, June 2008, p. 17. http://siteresources.worldbank.org/INTRUSSIANFEDERATION/Resources/rer16_Che2_Eng.pdf This correlation may be altering somewhat—recent price data shows that two indicators, the prices of West Texas and Brent Crude oil, long tied globally, are starting to diverge. But it is not clear why this is the case or whether it is epiphenomenal. See "Wide-Spread Confusion: What, Exactly Is the Price of Oil?" *The Economist*, 16 June 2011.

35. Larry Diamond, *The Spirit of Democracy: The Struggle to Build Free Societies Throughout the World*. New York: Henry Holt & Co., 2008, p. 76.

36. Alan B. Krueger and Jitka Maleckova, "Education, Poverty and Terrorism: Is There a Causal Connection?" *Journal of Economic Perspectives*, 17(4), Fall 2003, 119–144. See also Scott Helfstein, Nassir Abdullah, and Muhammad al-Obaidi, "Deadly Vanguards: A Study of al-Qa'ida's Violence Against Muslims," Combating Terrorism Center at West Point, December 2009.

37. See Michael L. Ross, "Does Oil Hinder Democracy?" *World Politics*, 53:3, April 2001. Morton Halperin, Joe Siegel, and Michael Weinstein, *The Democracy Advantage: How Democracies Promote Prosperity and Peace*. New York: Routledge, 2004.

38. Paul Collier, "Natural Resources, Development and Conflict: Channels of Causation and Policy Interventions," Oxford University and the World Bank, 2003.

39. Yaroslav Trofimov, "U.S. Rebuilds Power Plant, Taliban Reap a Windfall," The Wall Street Journal, July 13, 2010.

40. John Robb, *Brave New War*. New Jersey: John Wiley & Sons, Inc., 2007, p. 80.

41. Hisham Zerrifi, et al., "Incorporating Stress in Electric Power Systems Reliability Models," *Energy Policy*, 35 (2007), 61–75.

42. Natural gas-fired combined heat and power is also becoming a source of distributed generation to the developing world, though it is not renewable.

43. While distributed generation generally refers to electrical systems, the same concept can be applied to transportation, heating, and cooling systems to encourage locally produced, non-oil–based energy sources. We are interested in all energy provision to the developing world, since heating, food-preparation, and transport all play a role in the problems we mention earlier in this chapter. However, this book's primary focus is on electricity.

44. Michael Wines, "Toiling in the Dark: Africa's Power Crisis," *The New York Times*, July 29, 2007. http://www.nytimes.com/2007/07/29/world/africa/29power.html?pagewanted=print

45. Thomas Friedman, *Hot, Flat, and Crowded*, New York: Farrar, Straus, & Giroux, 2008, p. 196.

46. Paul Collier, *The Bottom Billion*. Oxford: Oxford University Press, 2007.

47. Susan Rose-Ackerman, Corruption and Government: Causes, Consequences and Reform, Cambridge: Cambridge University Press, 1999, pp. 9–25.

48. Corruption in contracting occurs in every country—including those at the highest end of transparency indicators. But in places such as Paraguay, corruption in international construction contracts from

1954–1989 ranged from 10%–20%. See ibid., pp. 27–29.

49. See http://www.cipe.org/about/index.php.

50. Ashraf Ghani and Clare Lockhart, *Fixing Failed States*, Oxford: Oxford University Press, 2008, pp. 205–208.

51. Robert Putnam, *Making Democracy Work: Civic Traditions in Modern Italy*. Princeton: Princeton University Press, 1994.

52. "No Strings Attached: The Case for a Distributed Grid and a Low-Oil Future," *World Affairs*, September–October 2010, 66.

53. World Energy Outlook 2000, International Energy Agency, p. 38.

54. *The Next Four Billion*, p. 79. Energy Strategy Approach Paper, October 2009, pp. 12–13. The World Bank Group, Sustainable Development Network.

55. Michael V. Copland, "Products for the other 3 Billions," *cnnmoney. com*, April 1, 2009. http://money.cnn.com/2009/04/01/technology/copeland_developing.fortune/index.htm

56. Op. cit., note 56, pp. 77, 79, 82. Numbers are for 2005. A significant portion of that is for electricity alone: According to the same source, the world's poor spend about $38 billion a year just on kerosene for lighting.

57. Meghan Deichert et al., *Global Soft Drinks: Industry Profile*, February 22, 2006. *Strategic Management in a Global Context*. New York: Datamonitor Reports, Reference Code: 0199-0802 (May 2005); and Mmoma Ejiofor, "World's Best-Selling Makeup," *Forbes Magazine*. http://www.forbes.com/2006/02/08/best-selling-cosmetics_cx_me_0209feat_ls.html/

58. "Fog Paralyses North India," *The Times of India*, January 8, 2010. http://timesofindia.indiatimes.com/india/Fog-paralyses-north-India

59. Brazil—Electricity, U.S. Energy Information Administration: Independent Statistics and Analysis. http://www.eia.doe.gov/cabs/Brazil/Electricity.html. See also Amro Hassan, "Egypt: Government Looks to Nuclear Energy to Face Increasing Power Needs," *Los*

Angeles Times, August 11, 2010. http://latimesblogs.latimes.com/babylonbeyond/2010/08/egypt-government-turn-to-nuclear-energy-to-face-increasing-power-needs.html

60. "World Bank Lending for Large Dams: A Preliminary Review of Impacts," World Bank Independent Evaluation Group, 2001. http://lnweb90.worldbank.org/oed/oeddoclib.nsf/DocUNIDViewForJavaSearch/BB68E3AEED5D12A4852567F5005D8D95?opendocument

61. Op. cit, note 61.

62. "World Bank Lending for Large Dams: A Preliminary Review of Impacts." September 1996. http://lnweb90.worldbank.org/oed/oeddoclib.nsf/0/bb68e3aeed5d12a4852567f5005d8d95?OpenDocument

63. E. J. Woodhouse, *A Political Economy of International Infrastructure Contracting: Lessons from the IPP Experience*. Stanford, CA: Stanford University, Center for Environmental Science and Policy, Program on Energy and Sustainable Development, 2005.

64. Pierre Audinet, "Electricity Prices in India," Energy Prices and Taxes, International Energy Agency, 2nd Quarter, 2002, p. XII. See also Kelli Joseph, "The Politics of Power: Electricity Reform in India," *Energy Policy*, 38:1, 503–511. Andrew MacAskill and Kartikay Mehrotra, "World's Greatest Power Thieves Keep 400 Million Indians in Dark," *Bloomberg.com*, May 2011. http://www.bloomberg.com/news/2011-05-31/world-s-greatest-power-thieves-keep-400-million-indians-in-dark.html

65. Mark Gregory, "India Struggles with Power Theft," *BBC World Service*, March 15, 2006. http://news.bbc.co.uk/2/hi/business/4802248.stm The Indian government compensates power companies for some loss due to subsidization of fuels—but not for theft, and it is less forthcoming with funds for infrastructure investment.

66. Raghuram Dharmaraju, "India's Electricity Transmission and Distribution Losses," *Cleantech India*, July 16, 2008. http://cleantechindia.wordpress.com/2008/07/16/indias-electricity-transmission-and-distribution-losses/

67. James Woolsey, Rachel Kleinfeld, Chelsea Sexton, "No Strings Attached: The Case for a Distributed Grid and a Low-Oil Future," *World Affairs*, September–October 2010, 66.

68. "Great Hopes Are Gone," *Time Magazine*, January 10, 1983. http://www.time.com/time/magazine/article/0,9171,923275,00.htm

69. In 2005 a local operator purchased the plant and started operations; however, maintenance problems have plagued the plant, as have political difficulties gaining insurance, and the plant runs far below capacity.

70. "Increasing Energy Access in Developing Countries: The Role of Distributed Generation," U.S. Agency for International Development Bureau for Economic Growth, Agriculture and Trade (EGAT) Office of Energy (May 2004), p. 1.

71. Brian Min, "Who Gets Public Goods? Democracy and the Provision of Electrification in the Developing World," Working Paper: UCLA Dept. of Political Science, January 24, 2008.

72. "Renewable Energy in China: Township Electrification Program," National Renewable Energy Laboratory (NREL), April 2004.

73. "Renewable Energy and Rural Electricity Access Project," The World Bank, November 2006.

74. "REtoolkit: A Resource for Renewable Energy Development," The World Bank, June 2008, p. 159.

75. "Study on PV Market Chains in East Africa," The World Bank, Energy for Sustainable Development Africa (ESDA), October 2003, p. 11.

76. "Nepal." http://www.usaid.gov/policy/budget/cbj2004/asia_near_east/Nepal.pdf See also "Donor Aid Priorities for Peacebuilding in Nepal's Post-Peace Settlement Transition," International Alert, December 2006. See also "Focus on Peru: Practical Action working in Latin America." http://practicalaction.org/docs/region_latin_america/practicalaction_peru.pdf

77. Op. cit. note 54, Woolsey, Kleinfeld, Sexton, "No Strings Attached." "Sun Biofuels Invest $20 Million in Tanzania Jatropha Project," *Mongabay.com*. August 6, 2007. http://news.mongabay. com/bioenergy/2007/08/sun-biofuels-invests-20-million-in.html. A. A. Refaat, N. K. Attia, H. A. Sibak, S. T. El Sheltawy, G. I. ElDiwani, "Production optimization and quality assessment of biodiesel from waste vegetable oil," *International Journal of Environmental Science and Technology*, 5(1), 75–82, Winter 2008.

78. The World Bank studied the transaction costs of opening a business in developing countries, and has found significant correlations between such transaction costs and development. See "Time Required to Start a Business," data: http://data.worldbank.org/ indicator/IC.REG.DURS and then the anecdotal evidence of how this translates into development costs, for instance Aymo Brunetti, Gregory Kisunko, and Beatrice Weder, *Institutional Obstacles for Doing Business Data Description and Methodology of a Worldwide Private Sector Survey*, p. 37, The World Bank. 1997. http:// siteresources.worldbank.org/INTWBIGOVANTCOR/Resources/ wps1759.pdf

79. *The Next Four Billion*, p. 79; Energy Strategy Approach Paper, October 2009, pp. 12–13. The World Bank Group, Sustainable Development Network; "Small Hydro Power for Developing Countries," European Small Hydro Power Association http://www. esha.be/fileadmin/esha_files/documents/publications/publications/ Brochure_SHP_for_Developing_Countries.pdf

80. Jeff Haeni, personal interview, March 11, 2010.

81. See V. Rangan, J. A. Quelch, G. Herrero, and B. Barton, *Business Solutions for the Global Poor: Creating Social and Economic Value*. Wiley, 2007.

82. Gregory Warner, "The Schools the Taliban Won't Torch," *Washington Monthly*, December 2007. For similar findings in Mexico, see Terry Wilson, Michael Ross, and Arturo Romero Paredes, "Governance Related to Energy Applications at the Community Level for Sustainability," USAID, May 2006.

83. Op. cit, note 74.

84. Such a professional system requires more training, and more maintenance, as well as technical skill to design systems in which peak demand does not exceed peak production and cause the entire system to shut down. Thus, they are better-suited for regions where a trained workforce exists to maintain them. They can also attract the attention of corrupt local officials, who see thriving businesses with capital. Yet where they manage to function, they provide the closest mimicking of a centralized grid's positive attributes. "'Minigrids' Solve South Asia Power Crisis," *BBC News*, October 27, 2003. http://news.bbc.co.uk/2/hi/3209239.stm

85. According to the World Bank IFC/GEF publication Selling Solar (note 93), rental financing is not sustainable as a business model. However, they base this vast conclusion on a single case, based on a business that was not local to the country in which it operated (Honduras), that had chosen to operate in the most rural, and therefore most expensive communities, and it does not seem to us to be a standard-bearer for such a strong statement.

86. Yerina Mugica, "Distributed Solar Energy in Brazil: Fabio Rosa's Approach to Social Entrepreneurship," University of North Carolina's Kenan-Flagler School of Business case study.

87. Hisham Zerreffi, *Rural Electrification: Strategies for Distributed Generation*, Dordrecht: Springer, 2010. pp. 105–128.

88. Since these lending groups all require their initial capital to be returned, they are more likely to lend for a business investment in energy that can generate revenues allowing the loan to be repaid, than to households that have no such prospects.

89. Op. cit, note 89.

90. Both the World Bank and the International Energy Agency put global fuel subsidies somewhere in the range of $100–$200 billion.

91. See Killian Reiche, Bernard Tenenbaum, and Clemencia Torres de Mästle, "Electrification and Regulation: Principles for a Model

Law," Paper #18, The World Bank Group Energy and Mining Sector Board, July 2006.

92. Paul Polak, *Out of Poverty*. Berrett-Koehler Publishers, 2008. pp. 88–89.

93. Elisabeth Rosenthal, "Third-World Stove Soot Is Target in Climate Fight," The *New York Times*, April 15, 2009. http://www.nytimes. com/2009/04/16/science/earth/16degrees.html

94. Op. cit, note 74, REToolkit, p. 96.

95. Reid Heffner, Kenneth Kurani, and Tom Turrentine, "Effects of Vehicle Image in Gasoline-Hybrid Electric Vehicles," Institute of Transportation Studies, University of California Davis, April 2008.

96. Tom Vanderbilt, "Smooth, Segway," *Slate*, July 8, 2009. http://www. slate.com/id/2222487/

97. Erik Simanis, "At the Base of the Pyramid: When selling to poor consumers, companies need to begin by doing something basic: They need to create the market," *The Wall Street Journal*, October 26, 2009. http://online.wsj.com/article/SB10001424052970203946 9045743018026849477 32.html

98. Rosabeth Moss Kanter, Ann S. Moore, Daniel L. Vasella, "Transforming Giants: The Centential Global Business Summit," Harvard Business School, October 15, 2008. http://www.hbs.edu/ centennial/businesssummit/leadership/transforming-giants.pdf

99. "The Facts," *P&G Children's Safe Drinking Water*. http://www.csdw. org/csdw/the_facts.shtml For similar findings, also see "The Global Water Crisis, Water: Essential for Life," *United Nations*. http://www. un.org/works/sub2.asp?lang=en&s=19

100. Op. cit., note 97, Simanis, "At the Base of the Pyramid."

101. Obviously, the price of water is now hotly contested in the developing world, as more systems privatize, and as some water rights are controlled by mafia and criminal groups. The issue is not actually the overall cost of water, but the change in the cost of

water for a process that did not appear to alter the water.

102. Op. cit, note 97, Simanis, "At the Base of the Pyramid."

103. Seth Godin, "Marketing at the Bottom of the Pyramid," *Fast Company*, September 9, 2010. http://www.fastcompany. com/1687863/marketing-to-the-bottom-of-the-pyramid

104. Jamie Anderson and Costas Markides, "Strategic Innovation at the Base of the Pyramid," MIT/Sloan Management Review, Fall 2007, p. 87.

105. Ibid, 88.

106. Ibid, 87.

107. Dipal C. Barua, "Grameen Shakti: Pioneering and Expanding Green Energy Revolution to Rural Bangladesh." Proceedings of The 3rd Green Growth Policy Dialogue: Greening the Business and Making Environment a Business Opportunity; June 2007; Bangkok, Thailand. United Nations Economic and Social Commission.

108. Gunnar Camner, Caroline Pulver, and Emil Sjoblom, "What Makes a Successful Mobile Money Implementation? Learning from M-PESA in Tanzania and Kenya," p. 8. Groupe Speciale Mobile Assn. http://mobileactive.org/files/file_uploads/mpesa_ke_tz.pdf

109. Fiona Graham, "M-PESA: Kenya's Mobile Wallet Revolution," *BBC News*, November 22, 2010. http://mobilemoneyafrica. com/?p=2693

110. Op. cit., note 113, Camner, Pulver, Sjoblom, "What Makes a Successful Mobile Money Implementation?" p. 8.

111. Ibid, 3.

112. Ibid, 5.

113. Differences in culture and business model also mattered—theft is more common in Kenya, so a safer method had greater attraction. However, Tanzanians did use other products to transfer funds and tended to transfer funds using airtime on their cell phones, a clunkier method that often discounted the amount of "funds"

transferred, but did not require filling out financial forms and relied on a more extensive number of agents. In other words, Tanzanians were familiar with their cell phones and could modify their behavior to adapt—but jumping to financial services was too many steps with too little explanation.

114. Allen Hammond and C. K. Prahalad, "Selling to the Poor," *Foreign Policy*, May–June 2004, 30–37.

115. Ibid.

116. C. K. Prahalad and Allen Hammond, "Serving the World's Poor, Profitably," *Harvard Business Review*, 80(9), September 2002.

117. Is energy different than a cell phone or shampoo? Of course. Energy is a service, not a good. In effect, you rent your energy in the form of your utility bill, but you own your cell phone—at least in the developed world. Yet in the developing world, the lines between goods and services have become blurred. This blurring makes energy, a shampoo packet, and even a cell phone much more alike than anyone might normally expect. And therefore, there are lessons to be learned in the energy sector from how cell phones and shampoo have made themselves ubiquitous in the developing world.

118. Op. cit., note 116, Prahalad and Hammond, "Selling to the Poor."

119. Ibid.

120. Ricardo Sandoval, "Block by Block: How one of the world's largest companies builds loyalty among Mexico's poor," *Stanford Social Innovation Review*, Summer 2005, 37.

121. Ibid, 37.

122. Ibid, 36.

123. Ibid, 36.

124. Ibid, 36.

125. Keith Bradsher, "China Racing Ahead of U.S. in the Drive to Go Solar," The *New York Times*, August 24, 2009. http://www.nytimes.com/2009/08/25/business/energy-environment/25solar.html

126. Photovoltaic prices dropped by 40% in 2009–2010, and another 20% in 2011—trends that industry experts expect to continue.

127. Rajesh Chhabara, "Grameen's World Bank Deal Brings Solar Power to Bangladesh," ClimateChangeCorp.com, http://www. climatechangecorp.com/content.asp?ContentID=5283

128. Dipal C. Barua, "Grameen Shakti: Pioneering and Expanding Green Energy Revolution to Rural Bangladesh," Proceedings of The 3rd Green Growth Policy Dialogue: Greening the Business and Making Environment a Business Opportunity, June 2007; Bangkok, Thailand. United Nations Economic and Social Commission.

129. "Connecting Africa: How ICT is Transforming a Continent," The World Bank. p. 1. http://siteresources.worldbank.org/ EXTINFORMATIONANDCOMMUNICATIONAND TECHNOLOGIES/Resources/282822-1192592444071/ ConnectingAfricaBrochure-Final.pdf

130. Today, prepaid subscribers make up more than 50% of users in many emerging-market countries including Bangladesh, Brazil, China, Egypt, India, Indonesia, Mexico, Pakistan, Russia, South Africa, and Vietnam. "10 Facts about Mobile Markets in Developing Countries," Vital Wave Consulting, 2008. http://www. vitalwaveconsulting.com/pdf/10FactsMobile.pdf. See also Kas Kalba, "The Adoption of Mobile Phones in Emerging Markets: Global Diffusion and the Rural Challenge," *International Journal of Communications* (2008), 642.

131. Sara Corbett, "Can the Cellphone Help End Global Poverty?" The *New York Times*, April 13, 2008. http://www.nytimes. com/2008/04/13/magazine/13anthropology-t.html?pagewanted=all

132. Ibid.

133. Op. cit., note 128, Barua, "Grameen Shakti: Pioneering and Expanding Green Energy Revolution to Rural Bangladesh," p. 10.

134. Op. cit., note 131, Corbett, "Can the Cellphone Help End Global Poverty?"

135. Henry Chesbrough, Shane Ahern, Megan Finn, and Stephane

Guerraz, "Business Models for Technology in the Developing World," California Management Review, 48(3), Spring 2006, 51.

136. Op. cit., note 137, Corbett, "Can the Cellphone Help End Global Poverty?"

137. Op. cit., note 133, Barua, "Grameen Shakti: Pioneering and Expanding Green Energy Revolution to Rural Bangladesh," p. 8.

138. Op. cit., note 87, Zerriffi, *Rural Electrification: Strategies for Distributed Generation*, p. 109.

139. Ibid, 105.

140. "Fabio Rosa's approach to social entrepreneurship: Distributed solar energy in Brazil," World Business Council for Sustainable Development, Case Study, 2004. http://www.wbcsd.org/DocRoot/ CpKFwVJovi1DlJiJrrGw/ideaas_sta_full_case_final_web.pdf. See also op. cit., note 91, Zerriffi, Rural Electrification: Strategies for Distributed Generation, February 2010, pp. 78–108.

141. Yerina Mugica, "Distributed Solar Energy in Brazil: Fabio Rosa's Approach to Social Entrepreneurship," University of North Carolina Kenan-Flager Business School case study.

142. Op. cit., note 128, Barua, "Grameen Shakti: Pioneering and Expanding Green Energy Revolution to Rural Bangladesh," p.6.

143. For further explanation of the importance of this phenomenon, see op. cit., note 92, Paul Polak, *Out of Poverty: What Works When Traditional Approaches Fail*, p. 45.

144. Jamie Anderson and Costas Markides, "Strategic Innovation at the Base of the Pyramid," *MIT/ Sloan Management Review*, 49(1), Fall 2007, p. 86. See also Malcolm Foster, "Cell Phones Vital in Developing World," *The Washington Post*, January 27, 2007. http:// www.washingtonpost.com/wp-dyn/content/article/2007/01/27/ AR2007012700662_pf.html. See also Ross Biddiscombe, "Mobile phone information network gives Indian farmers new hope," Guardian.com, June 18, 2010. http://www.guardian.co.uk/activate/ mobile-phone-indian-farmers-hope

145. "Vodaphone: Focus on a Member, January 2008," CSR Europe. http://www.csreurope.org/pages/en/focus_vodafone.html

146. Ibid.

147. Op. cit., note 127, Chhabara, "Grameen's World Bank deal brings solar power to Bangladesh."

148. Op. cit., note 55, Copeland, "Products for the other 3 Billion," *cnnmoney*.com, April 1, 2009. http://money.cnn.com/2009/04/01/technology/copeland_developing.fortune/index.htm

149. Op. cit., note 55, Copeland, "Can the Cellphone Help End Global Poverty?"

150. Op. cit., note 55, Copeland, "Products for the other 3 Billion."

151. "Rural Energy Foundation." http://www.ruralenergy.nl/

152. Ashden Awards 2010 documentary developed to highlight REF's efforts in sub-Saharan Africa. "Documentary: Rural Energy Foundation, African villages lit up by solar power—Ashden Award winner." http://www.youtube.com/watch?v=ZHVDm-B_l4g&feature=related

153. Ibid.

154. Ibid.

155. Ibid.

156. Ibid.

157. Ibid.

158. Ibid.

159. "Case study summary: Rural Energy Foundation (REF), Sub-Saharan Africa," 2010 Ashden Award for Africa. http://www.ashdenawards.org/files/reports/REF%20case%20study.pdf

160. Op. cit., note 152, Documentary: Rural Energy Foundation, African villages lit up by solar power—Ashden Award winner.

161. Ibid.

162. Ashden Awards 2007 documentary developed to highlight Zara Solar's efforts to provide lighting in the Mwanza region of Tanzania. "Documentary: Zara Solar Ltd., Tanzania, Affordable rural solar PV energy—Ashden Award winner." http://www.youtube.com/watch?v=SHgXR2cmVyA

163. Anne Wheldon and Mike Pepler, "Zara Solar Ltd., Tanzania: Providing affordable solar systems in Northern Tanzania," Ashden Awards, May 2007. http://www.ashdenawards.org/files/reports/Zara_2007_Technical_report.pdf

164. Ibid.

165. Op. cit., note 162, Documentary: Zara Solar Ltd., Tanzania

166. E+Co is a nonprofit, but part of a new movement of business–social sector hybrid organizations. It expects its loans to be paid back with interest. While its mission allows it to gain lower returns than a purely profit-minded venture capital firm, it is an excellent example of a profitable triple-bottom line business, or socially responsible business, that does well by doing good. See http://eandco.net/index.php?cID=84

167. "Zara Solar-Case Study," Increasing Energy Access Through Enterprise, USAID. http://energyaccess.wikispaces.com/Zara+Solar+-+Case+Study#overview

168. Ibid.

169. The project set a target of 1,682 solar home systems sold over the course of five years. As of the conclusion of the project in June 2009, more than 8,000 systems were being sold per year. Information listed on project website. "Transformation of the Rural Photovoltaic Market in Tanzania." http://www.solarmwanza.org/

170. Isdory Fitwangile and Eric K. Mugurusi, "2009 Annual Performance Report (APR)/ Project Implementation Review (PIR): Transformation of the Rural Photovoltaic (PV) Market in Tanzania," UNDP/GEF, June 26, 2009, p. 5. http://www.

solarmwanza.org/APR_PIR_Mwanza_PV_2009-climate%20 change%20reporting.pdf

171. Mohamed Ali Hamid and Finias Magessa, "Transformation of Rural Photovoltaic Market in Tanzania Project—Terminal Evaluation Report," August 2009, p. 32. erc.undp.org/evaluationadmin/ downloaddocument.html?docid=3244

172. Ibid., p. 33.

173. Op. cit., note 129, "Connecting Africa: How ICT Is Transforming a Continent," The World Bank.

174. Op. cit., note 89, "Selling Solar: Lessons from More than a Decade of IFC's Experience," p. 18.

175. Op. cit., note 128, Barua, "Grameen Shakti: Pioneering and Expanding Green Energy Revolution to Rural Bangladesh."

176. Op. cit., note 89, "Selling Solar: Lessons from More than a Decade of IFC's Experience," p. 21.

177. Wolfgang Mostert, Kristina Johnson, and John MacLean, *Publicly Backed Guarantees as Policy Instruments to Promote Clean Energy.* Basel, Switzerland: United Nations Environment Programme, Sustainable Energy Finance Alliance; DB Climate Change Advisors, 2011. See also *GET FiT Plus: De-risking clean energy business models in a developing country context*, Chapter IV. New York, NY: The Deutsche Bank Group.

178. Op. cit., note 89, "Selling Solar: Lessons from More than a Decade of IFC's Experience," p. 15.

179. Op. cit., note 89, "Selling Solar: Lessons from More than a Decade of IFC's Experience," p. 30.

180. Op. cit., note 89, "Selling Solar: Lessons from More than a Decade of IFC's Experience," pp. 40–44.

181. Op. cit., note 129, "Connecting Africa: How ICT Is Transforming a Continent," p. 1.

182. Ibid., 11, 26.

183. Op. cit., note 89, "Selling Solar: Lessons from More than a Decade of IFC's Experience," p. 23.

184. Op. cit., note 127, Chhabara, "Grameen's World Bank deal brings solar power to Bangladesh."

185. For an example of how Bangladeshi politicians killed the treadle-pump market that was helping the poorest of the poor farmers, see op. cit., note 96, Paul Polak, *Out of Poverty*, p. 36.

186. Polak, who helped to found Stanford's Design for Extreme Affordability course, provides guidelines for designing for the poor in *Out of Poverty*, pp. 75–79, op. cit., note 92.

187. A McKinsey study found that in 2007, $3.2 billion in venture capital and private equity fueled new competitors to enter this emerging sector. Peter Lorenz, Dickon Pinner, and Thomas Seitz, "The Economics of Solar Power," McKinsey Quarterly, June 2008, p. 15.

188. Op. cit., note 55, Copland, "Products for the other 3 Billions."

189. A similar success story from the same class is ApproTEC's (now Kickstart's) irrigation pump in Kenya: http://stanford.edu/group/AIM/AIMPrograms/EventsArchives/IAC404/Aaron.pdf

190. The larger solar market created in developed countries by feed-in tariffs and similar policies convinced many manufacturers to move toward production that meets higher load requirements. This brought down the price of solar components for these markets, but left market prices higher for developing countries needing the same raw materials, but now facing a smaller manufacturing sector. Between mid-2005 and the end of 2006, the price of 40-watt panels most demanded by the developing world increased by 50%, and 20-watt panels increased by 36%. See, op. cit., note 89, "Selling Solar: Lessons from More than a Decade of IFC's Experience," pp. 11, 19.

191. Op. cit., note 93, "Selling Solar: Lessons from More than a Decade of IFC's Experience," p. 22.

192. Ibid., 25.

193. An Interview with Professor Muhammad Yunus, Chairman, Grameen Shakti, June 4, 2010. http://www.gshakti.org/index. php?option=com_content&view=article&id=119&Itemid=121

194. Op. cit., note 128, Barua, "Grameen Shakti: Pioneering and Expanding Green Energy Revolution to Rural Bangladesh," p. 9.

195. Afghan Clean Energy Program (ACEP), concept paper, January 2009.

196. Peter Meisen, "Rural Electrification in Afghanistan: How do we electrify the villages of Afghanistan?" Global Energy Network Institute, March 2003.

197. While the widely cited UN and USAID numbers on deforestation are deeply flawed, the forest used for wood harvesting is depleting at a serious rate. See: Harry R. Bader et al., "The Afghanistan Timber Trade: An Evaluation of the Interaction Between the Insurgency, GIRoA, and Criminality in the Task Force Bastogne Area of Operations," Natural Resources Counterinsurgency Cell, Joint Civ-Mil team, July 21, 2010, pp. 7–9. Approximately 80% of all Afghan cooking uses wood; however, as cited earlier, distributed generation of electricity is unlikely to affect this problem—although solar cookers could, in the same way that wood gassification, discussed later, is a distributed energy (rather than electricity) technology that could affect fuel usage for heat.

198. For instance, Rory Donohoe, USAID field program officer for Helmand, described how after electricity was brought to the province, the number of ice-making factories quadrupled, and the local marble polishing plant was able to institute three shifts a day instead of one, providing employment for many more Afghans. Yaroslav Trofimov, "U.S. Rebuilds Power Plant, Taliban Reap a Windfall," The *Wall Street Journal*, July 13, 2010. http://online.wsj.com/article/SB1000142 405274870454500457535299424274701 2.html

199. Vijay Modi, Susan McDade, Dominique Lallement, and Jamal Saghir, "Energy Services for the Millennium Development Goals,"

2005, p. 18. Also see Makoto Kanagawa and Toshihiko Nakata, "Analysis of the Energy Access Improvement in Developing Countries through Rural Electrification," 25th Annual North American Conference of the USAEE/IAEE Colorado, USA, September 2005, slide 13. http://www.iaee.org/documents/denver/kanagawa.pdf

200. Andrew Tilghman, "Illiteracy, Desertion Slow Afghan Training," *ArmyTimes.com*, August 24, 2010. http://www.armytimes.com/news/2010/08/military-afghan-army-illiteracy-082310w/

201. Ibid.

202. "Sustain the Mission Project: Casualty Factors for Fuel and Water Resupply Convoys," Army Environmental Policy Institute Report, September 2009, p. i.

203. The Associated Press, "Trucks with Fuel for War Set Ablaze in Pakistan," *The New York Times*, October 3, 2010. http://www.nytimes.com/2010/10/04/world/asia/04pstan.html

204. Elizabeth Rosenthal, "US Military Orders Less Dependence of Fossil Fuels," *The New York Times*, October 4, 2010. http://www.nytimes.com/2010/10/05/science/earth/05fossil.html?_r=1

205. The $400 figure for the fully burdened cost of fuel has been cited by individuals such as General Kern, and General Conway, Commandant of the Marine Corps. The actual number differs, of course, by the delivery to a position on the battlefield. The issue was first discussed by the Defense Science Board Task Force on DoD Energy Strategy, "More Fight—Less Fuel," February 2008.

206. "Securing Afghanistan's Future: Accomplishments and the Strategic Path Forward," January 2004, p. 3.

207. "Power Sector Strategy for the Afghanistan National Development Strategy (with Focus on Prioritization)," Ministry of Energy and Water of the Islamic Republic of Afghanistan, May 2007, p. 2.

208. These resources were all exploited during the period of Soviet control in the 1980s, and some began to be developed beforehand.

See Saeed Parto and Asif Karimi, "Afghanistan's Power Sector: Pipedreams or Workable Solutions," Afghanistan Public Policy Research Organization Policy Paper, August 2007.

209. Finding reliable numbers on Afghan energy is, as might be expected, difficult. The EIA suggests that Afghanistan has proven reserves of 1.75 trillion cubic *feet*—but these are not necessarily exploitable. The numbers we use here are drawn from Parto and Karimi, "Afghanistan's Power Sector: Pipedreams or Workable Solutions," op. cit., note 208, pp. 2, 10–11.

210. Op. cit., note 198, Trofimov, "U.S. Rebuilds Power Plant, Taliban Reap a Windfall."

211. Op. cit., note 8, Zorpette, "Struggling for Power in Afghanistan."

212. Op. cit., note 2, Blackledge, Riechmann, and Lardner, "After Years of Rebuilding, Most Afghans Lack Power: A U.S. Led Effort Could Do More Harm than Good."

213. Urban Population (Percent of Total Population Living in Urban Areas) 2009, World Bank Development Indicators, http://data. worldbank.org/indicator/SP.URB.TOTL.IN.ZS

214. Liz Alden Wily, "Looking for Peace on the Pastures: Rural Land Relations in Afghanistan," Afghanistan Research and Evaluation Unit, December 2004, p. 8.

215. "Afghanistan," World Statistics Pocketbook, United Nations Statistics Division. http://data.un.org/CountryProfile.aspx

216. Hisham Zerriffi, Hadi Dowlatabad, and Alex Farrell, "Incorporating Stress in Electric Power Systems Stress Reliability Models," *Energy Policy*, 35 (2007), 61–75.

217. Op. cit., note 198, Trofimov, "U.S. Rebuilds Power Plant, Taliban Reap a Windfall."

218. Ibid.

219. Op. cit., note 208, Parto and Karimi, "Afghanistan's Power Sector: Pipedreams or Workable Solutions," p. 11.

220. "National Solidarity Program: A Hidden Success," Institute for State Effectiveness, 2008, pp. 1–2.

221. "The A to Z Guide to Afghanistan Assistance 2009," Afghanistan Research and Evaluation Unit (AREU), p. 51.

222. "Assessment & Recommendations for the Sustainable Implementation of Micro Hydro Power Projects in Afghanistan," Entec AG Consulting & Engineering, February 2006.

223. Linton Wells, "Distributed Infrastructure in Afghan Reconstruction and Stabilization," unpublished White Paper from STAR-TIDES, February 21, 2009, p. 5.

224. Tobias Becker, "Renewable Energy Supply for Rural Areas (ESRA)," GTZ Energy Programme Afghanistan, 2007.

225. Ben Arnoldy, "Afghanistan War: How USAID Loses Hearts and Minds," *Christian Science Monitor*, July 28, 2010. http://www.csmonitor.com/World/Asia-South-Central/2010/0728/Afghanistan-war-How-USAID-loses-hearts-and-minds

226. Op. cit., note 223, Wells, "Distributed Infrastructure in Afghan Reconstruction and Stabilization," p. 3.

227. Op. cit., note 223, "Assessment & Recommendations for the Sustainable Implementation of Micro Hydro Power Projects in Afghanistan," p. 4.

228. Op. cit., note 228, Wells, "Distributed Infrastructure in Afghan Reconstruction and Stabilization," p. 10.

229. As an illustration, one of our authors offers her experience of a journey from Kabul to Bamiyan in 2005, a distance of just over 100 miles that took nine hours by jeep, and yielded four flat tires.

230. Op. cit., note 208, Parto and Karimi, "Afghanistan's Power Sector: Pipedreams or Workable Solutions," p. 7.

231. Op. cit., note 187, Peter Lorenz, Dickon Pinner, and Thomas Seitz, "The Economics of Solar Power," McKinsey Quarterly, June 2008, p. 7.

232. See op. cit., note, note 92, Polak, *Out of Poverty*, pp. 146–148, for guidelines on creating private-sector supply chains that bring the most value to the poorest members of the chain.

233. For more on Ashoka's work on hybrid value chains, see "Hybrid Value Chain Format." http://fec.ashoka.org/content/hybrid-value-chain-framework

234. Blackledge, Riechmann, and Lardner, "After Years of Rebuilding, Most Afghans Lack Power."

235. "Poverty Reduction and Rural Renewable Energy Development: A Discussion Paper," ADB TA 4461, Asian Development Bank, 2006, p. 6.

236. Ministry of Energy and Water, "Power Sector Strategy for the Afghanistan National Development Strategy," Ministry of Energy and Water of the Islamic Republic of Afghanistan, 2007, quoted in Hisham Zerriffi, "Briefing Paper: Alternative Electrification Options for Afghanistan," February 2008, p. 2.

237. Op. cit., note 10, Trofimov, "Cell Carriers Bow to Taliban Threat."

238. Laura King, "Taliban's New Strategy Is Pushing the Wrong Buttons," *Los Angeles Times*, April 23, 2008. http://articles.latimes.com/2008/apr/23/world/fg-cellphones23

239. Op. cit., note 10, Trofimov, "Cell Carriers Bow to Taliban Threat."

240. In Africa, distributed generation is starting to blossom precisely because of the spread of cell phones. A *New York Times* page one story describes how a woman decided to purchase solar panels to avoid her regular, multi-hour walk to a business that charged phones, which was so overwhelmed that customers needed to leave their phones for three days for charging. With her solar panels, she was running a similar phone-charging business for her neighborhood, but did not expect the extra income to last long, given the flood of neighbors buying their own distributed generation systems to charge their own phones! See Elizabeth Rosenthal, "African Huts Far from the Grid Glow with Renewable Power," *The New York Times*, December 24, 2010. http://www.

nytimes.com/2010/12/25/science/earth/25fossil.html

241. D. F. Barnes and J. Halpern, Subsidies and Sustainable Rural Energy Services: Can We Create Incentives Without Distorting Markets?, Washington, D.C.: Joint UNDP/World Bank Energy Sector Management Assistance Programme (ESMAP), 2000. p. 13.

242. Ashraf Ghani and Clare Lockhart, *Fixing Failed States*, Oxford: Oxford University Press, 2008. pp. 205–208.

243. Robert Putnam, *Making Democracy Work: Civic Traditions in Modern Italy*. Princeton: Princeton University Press, 1994.

244. Op. cit., note 223, Wells, "Distributed Infrastructure in Afghan Reconstruction and Stabilization," p. 5. In Bangladesh, Grameen Shakti also found that when technology was owned by the beneficiaries, they took greater responsibility for proper maintenance and use. See, op. cit., note 128, Barua, "Grameen Shakti: Pioneering and Expanding Green Energy Revolution to Rural Bangladesh."

245. Op. cit., note 204, Rosenthal, "U.S. Military Orders Less Dependence on Fossil Fuels."

246. The Naval Postgraduate School (NPS) at Monterey, California, in conjunction with the US Special Operations Command (SOCOM) is testing renewable energy technologies. It held the first tests in the winter of 2009, and continues to test such equipment for deployment to the field. See, op. cit., note 223, Wells, "Distributed Infrastructure in Afghan Reconstruction and Stabilization," p. 4.

247. Seth G. Jones, "Stabilization from the Bottom Up," Testimony presented before the Commission on Wartime Contracting, the RAND Corporation, February 22, 2010. http://www.rand.org/content/dam/rand/pubs/testimonies/2010/RAND_CT340.pdf

248. Bill Reichart is managing director of Garage Technology Ventures. Op. cit., note 55, Copland, "Products for the other 3 Billions."

249. Op. cit., note 89, "Selling Solar: Lessons from More than a Decade of IFC's Experience," p. 13.

250. Op. cit., note 241. See also V. Radulovic, "Are New Institutional Economics Enough? Promoting Photovoltaics in India's Agricultural Sector," Energy Policy 33, 2005: 1883–1899. See also UNEP, Reforming Energy Subsidies: An Explanatory Summary of the Issues and Challenges, United Nations Environment Programme, 2002.